# ERIC THEISS

Post Hill
PRESS

A POST HILL PRESS BOOK
ISBN: 978-1-64293-742-8
ISBN (eBook): 978-1-64293-743-5

Toss & Go!™:
Featuring Quick & Easy Pressure Cooker & Slow Cooker Recipes
© 2021 by Eric Theiss
All Rights Reserved

Post Hill Press
New York • Nashville
posthillpress.com

Published in the United States of America

1  2  3  4  5  6  7  8  9  10

# ACKNOWLEDGMENTS

This book could not have happened without some close
and much appreciated colleagues.

Big thanks go out to Claire Winslow, who once again made the recipe-
writing process much more fun and functional, and to Jeannette
Mostowicz for her awesome food styling.

Thank you also to Parker Bliss for overseeing this book project from start
to finish, and to photographer Matt Wagemann and his assistant, Mike
Levi, whose photography brought these recipes to life on the page.

Thank you to Chef Kris Amerine, who has been putting up with me since
the Meritage days! And thank you to Post Hill, Anthony Ziccardi, Michael
Wilson, and your amazing team for your vision and stellar work. Lastly
thank you to Linda Lisco for your help as a colleague and friend.

**Eric Theiss**

# TABLE OF CONTENTS

## SOUP & STEWS

## PASTA, RICE & RISOTTO

# POULTRY

# BEEF, PORK & LAMB

# SEAFOOD

## POTATO & VEGETABLE

## DESSERTS

# ABOUT THE AUTHOR

Today, Eric Theiss is known for his inventive cooking and creative flair as America's favorite TV host and chef and a top-selling cookbook author. Seen regularly as the Copper Chef, Eric also hosts several other award-winning infomercials featuring new and innovative PowerXL products.

However, Eric's love of cooking began as a child in New Jersey in his Italian mother's kitchen. Under her guidance he began a life of culinary exploration. In his twenties his love of food, wine, and fine dining led him to work in numerous restaurant kitchens, leading him to more formal training at The Culinary Renaissance under the acclaimed chef, Frank Falcinelli. In 1997, Eric went on to create his own fine dining restaurant and bar, Meritage, in Pennsylvania. Meritage earned rave reviews from diners and prominent Philadelphia food critics. There his restaurant dream was realized.

Always loving to roam Meritage's tables and speak with diners, Eric discovered that home cooks shared his love of cooking but help was needed to make home cooking more simple and accessible. There his interest in kitchen product innovation began, and Eric began working with kitchen brands and retailers. For the past 15 years, Eric has appeared on TV shopping networks, broadcast and cable TV showcasing both his own collections of kitchen equipment and cookbooks as well as others' and even assisting celebrity chefs in the development and marketing of their brands.

Eric has written 10 cookbooks selling over 500k books. He is thrilled to launch Toss & Go!, a series of cookbooks focused on easy, time-saving cooking from a professional chef who knows the secrets inside and out.

Eric currently lives in Pennsylvania with his brilliant wife Jessica and two teenage sons Cameron and Maxwell. Their cats PoePoe, Whitman, and Ginger are adored by all!

# PRESSURE COOKER Q&A

**Q: Are pressure cookers safe?**

A: The short answer is yes! The new pressure cookers, especially the electric pressure cookers, are extremely safe. They have several safety features built in to avoid clogging and overheating. In most cases, the new electric pressure cookers will turn off the heat supply if temperatures get too high. Thanks to the cycling of heat in electric pressure cookers, there is no need for the constant, frightening screeching of the old fashioned "jiggle valves" found on older manual pressure cookers. The modern-day electric pressure cookers have many built-in safety features that prevent pressure build up if the lid is not closed properly and they also prevent the lid from opening until all pressure has been released.

**Q: How long have pressure cookers been in existence?**

A: While pressure cookers were first invented in the 1600's, they didn't become a common household item until the beginning of the 20th Century. Pressure cookers were originally called "steam digesters" when invented by physicist Denis Papin in London. The first pressure cookers sold commercially were made from tinned cast iron. Now, the best pressure cookers are made of stainless steel. The first pressure cooker cookbook was published in Spain in 1924 and included 360 recipes specifically for the cooker.

**Q: Do pressure cookers use more energy?**

A: No, thanks to the efficiency of pressure cooking. Using only a small amount of energy to maintain pressure is the key. Cooking time is faster—often 1/3 to ½ the amount of traditional cooking times—and your kitchen remains much cooler.

**Q: Are pressure cookers hard to cook in?**

A: NO! In fact, they are very easy to cook in. In most cases, it is just a matter of putting at least a cup of liquid and your ingredients into the cooker, locking the lid and choosing a cook time. What's nice about cooking in a modern electric pressure cooker is that you don't need to stand around and tend to the food as it cooks. You literally walk away and let it do its job!

**Q: Are pressure cookers hard to clean?**

A: No, for a few reasons. Most electric pressure cookers are nonstick. The inner pot is easily removed and because you are cooking under super heat and steam, you rarely have a baked-on mess. Most pressure cooker meals are cooked in one pot all at once, so there are fewer pans to clean. Splatter is eliminated thanks to the lid, which is locked on during cooking.

**Q: Why is pressure cooking so much faster than traditional cooking?**

A: The answer can be long and boring, but it's actually very simple. Pressure cooking raises the temperature of the liquid from a 212° F boiling point, up to approximately 240° F. It may not sound like much, but being able to cook at higher heat enables faster cooking—in some cases, up to 70% faster.

**Q: If cooking in a pressure cooker is hotter than traditional cooking, does that mean that all of the nutrients are destroyed?**

A: No, pressure cooking nutrition has been studied for a long time, and in many cases pressure cooking will retain more nutrients than traditional methods. Cooking foods for less time at higher temperatures is easier on nutrients, vitamins and minerals than the stovetop or the oven. Boiling vegetables, for example, causes the nutrients to leach out into the water and escape through steam vapor. Then we dump the water with the nutrients down the drain. Pressure cookers trap the steam and the nutrients inside the pot. One 2007 study published in the Journal of Food and Science showed that broccoli maintained 92% of its Vitamin C when pressure cooked, as opposed to the 78% that was maintained through boiling the broccoli. There have also been studies to show that pressure cooking can make many hard-to-digest foods easier to digest.

**Q: Is pressure cooking healthy?**

A: In many cases, no fats or oils are needed to create great tasting food, which creates leaner, lighter results. Also, because pressure cooking is so fast and easy, it makes it less likely that you will need to order unhealthy take out or fast food after a long day or when you are in a pinch for time.

**Q: Is pressure cooking environmentally friendly?**

A: More than ever, people are seeking out healthy alternatives and whole foods. Pressure cookers make it easy to cook whole foods, and you retain a higher percentage of the nutrients when pressure cooking. Also, because it takes less time to cook under pressure, we are using less power resources to cook. Saving energy is good for the environment, and for your bills.

**Q: What is a gasket and why is it an important part of the pressure cooker?**

A: The lid of the pressure cooker is lined with a flexible (rubber or silicone) ring that goes around the entire circumference of the lid and allows the lid to create an airtight seal. It is important to make sure you clean and dry the gasket after each use. Follow your instruction manual so that you remove the gasket properly. Your gasket should last many years, but if it ever appears dried out, cracked or stiffened, you should replace it. Most manufacturers will recommend replacing your gasket annually if you pressure cook regularly.

**Q: What do they mean by "quick release" and "natural release" when releasing the pressure in my pressure cooker?**

A: Most pressure cookers come equipped with a pressure regulator that is built into the lid. These valves release excess pressure in the event of a malfunction. Every pressure cooker recipe ends with either a "quick release," when you manually open the pressure valve and let the steam out quickly or "natural release," when you simply turn off the cooker and let the steam escape gradually and naturally without opening the valve manually. Just follow the recipe instructions to know which is best for which recipe.

**Q: What makes pressure-cooked food so tasty?**

A: Pressure cookers are renowned for creating super tasty meals in less time. That's because super-heated steam pounds the food with pressure while the flavors and ingredients cannot escape the unit. Because all of the goodness stays inside the cooker, the food comes out with intense flavor. Beyond that, cuts of meat that contain the most flavor tend to be the ones that are usually tougher to make tender through cooking. The pressure cooker cooks at higher temperatures, so that breaks down the meat quickly, making it juicy and fall-apart tender.

**Q: Can I brown or "sear" my food in a pressure cooker?**

A: As with the Power Pressure Cooker XL, most electric pressure cookers have a browning or searing mode. In the PPCXL, you simply turn the unit on and push any one of the pre-set cooking buttons to put the unit into browning mode. Once the food and liquid are added and the lid is locked, the unit switches to pressure cooking mode. Other brands of pressure cookers may have buttons labeled "browning" or "searing" mode.

**Q: Can I steam in the pressure cooker?**

A: YES! Many electric pressure cookers come with a steaming rack, and all you have to do is pour water into the pot and using the steaming rack, place the ramekins, ceramic dish, or even metal baker onto the rack.

**Q: Can I put frozen foods into my pressure cooker?**

A: Yes. Just remember to add an extra 10 minutes for frozen meats.

**Q: How long will it take the pressure cooker to come to pressure and start cooking?**

A: This can take anywhere from a few minutes to up to 17 minutes, depending on the ingredients and the amount of liquid in the cooker and the temperature of the ingredients. For instance, frozen raw wings will take longer to pressurize than the same amount of raw thawed wings, etc.

**Q: If there is steam coming out of my lid, is that normal?**

A: No. If there is steam coming out of the sides of your pressure cooker and the pressure valve is in the closed position, then the lid has not sealed correctly. This sometimes happens when the unit is new. Check that your gasket ring is in place. Also, try pushing down on the lid to create the tight seal and stop the steam from escaping. Check your instruction manual for further troubleshooting ideas. The only time steam should escape the cooker is when the cooking is finished and the steam is releasing from the pressure release valve.

# SLOW COOKER Q&A

**Q: Why use a slow cooker?**

A: Slow cooking has been a time-honored way to cook for your family because it allows you the ability to put ingredients into a pot and then essentially "leave it" to cook at a low temperature for a few hours or even several hours, depending on what you're cooking. This easy method of cooking generally creates comfort food that has marinated for a long time in the pot and is ready to eat when you are. Slow cooking eliminates the need for stirring periodically and is known for being easy and relaxing.

**Q: Is slow cooking safe?**

A: YES. Because slow cookers bring the food up to a safe temperature relatively quickly, there is no chance for bacterial growth. Bacteria grows between 4° and 140°, but slow cookers do not stay at those low temperatures. They get into the higher temperatures quickly enough to totally prevent any food safety issues.

**Q: Can I use any recipe in a slow cooker?**

A: Yes, but often it's important to cut down on the amount of liquid that the recipe calls for, since the rate of evaporation is much lower in a slow cooker with a lid on than in the oven or on the stovetop.

**Q: Is slow cooking only for soups and stews?**

A: No! Although slow cookers are known mainly for those types of dishes, you can cook many foods in a slow cooker, including side dishes, breads and desserts!

**Q: Can I brown in a slow cooker?**

A: Generally you do have to brown or sear your meat in a separate pan or skillet prior to the slow cooking process; however, if you have a multi-cooker or a pressure cooker that has a slow cooker function, you can often sear or brown prior to choosing the slow cooking function.

**Q: Do foods get mushy in the slow cooker since it cooks for so long?**

A: Not necessarily, and to prevent overcooking certain foods like pasta or instant rice, add those during the last 30 minutes or so of your cooking time. Vegetables and meat take longer to cook.

**Q: Can I slow cook in the oven or on the stovetop even if I don't have a "slow cooker" or a "pressure cooker?"**

A: YES! Use your favorite Dutch oven (any pot that holds about 4-6 quarts of liquid and has a good fitting lid). The tight fitting lid is very important to keep the steam in the pot. If you choose the stovetop, you will need to stir occasionally and check the heat under the burner to make sure that the food on the bottom of the pan isn't burning or sticking. I prefer slow cooking in the oven for that reason.

**Q: How to convert "slow cooker" recipes to oven braising/slow cooking.**

A: There is no surefire way to convert. My experience is that an oven set between 250°F and 275°F works great. Always pre-heat the oven, brown your meat, and bring your liquids to a boil on the stovetop prior to putting the pot in the oven. One rule of thumb is to double the time it takes to cook your recipe at 350°F. Unless I am cooking a large piece of meat (like a 6 lb. roast), I have never needed more than 4 hours in the oven to hit the proper internal temperature. (Please consult internal temperature chart in this book). It's also important to be sure your oven is calibrated properly.

**Q: What are some helpful tips for slow cooking in the oven?**

A: Always remember to be sure your lid is secure. Be sure to use plenty of liquid so that evaporation doesn't ruin your recipe. You should check periodically and add more liquid as needed. If it's a large roast, it's a good idea to flip it about halfway through to be sure that the protein is cooked in the liquid most of the time.

**Q: Why isn't my sauce very concentrated when I slow cook?**

A: Because you are cooking slowly and with a lid most of the time, you retain most of the liquid during the cooking process, which doesn't lend itself to a rich, concentrated gravy or sauce. This can be remedied by setting aside the meat or protein at the end and "reducing" the liquid on the stovetop over medium heat without a lid until you've reached the desired consistency (or the gravy or sauce coats a spoon).

# EQUIVALENCY CHARTS

## Dry (Weight) Measurements

| Misc.* | Teaspoons | Tablespoons | Ounces | Cups | Grams | Pounds |
|---|---|---|---|---|---|---|
| 1 dash | $1/16$ tsp. | - | - | - | - | - |
| 1 pinch/6 drops | $1/8$ tsp. | - | - | - | - | - |
| 15 drops | ¼ tsp. | - | - | - | - | - |
| 1 splash | ½ tsp. | - | - | - | - | - |
| - | 1 tsp. | $1/3$ tbsp. | $1/6$ oz | - | - | - |
| - | 3 tsp. | 1 tbsp. | ½ oz | - | 14.3 g | - |
| - | - | 2 tbsp. | 1 oz | $1/8$ cup | 28.3 g | - |
| - | - | 4 tbsp. | 2 oz | ¼ cup | 56.7 g | - |
| - | - | 5 $1/3$ tbsp. | 2.6 oz | $1/3$ cup | 75.6 g | - |
| - | - | 8 tbsp. | 4 oz | ½ cup | 113.4 g | - |
| - | - | 12 tbsp. | 6 oz | ¾ cup | 170.1 g | - |
| - | - | 16 tbsp. | 8 oz | 1 cup | 226.8 g | ½ lb |
| - | - | 32 tbsp. | 16 oz | 2 cups | 453.6 g | 1 lb |
| - | - | 64 tbsp. | 32 oz | 4 cups/1 qt. | 907.2 g | 2 lb |

* Dash, pinch, drop, and splash are subjective measurements that have no formally agreed-upon definition.

# Abbreviations

| Term | Dry & Liquid | Abbreviation |
|------|--------------|--------------|
| cup | usually liquid | - |
| fluid ounce | only liquid | fl oz. |
| gallon | dry or liquid | - |
| inch | - | in. |
| ounce | dry | oz. |
| pint | dry or liquid | - |
| pound | dry | lb |
| quart | dry or liquid | qt./qts. |
| teaspoon | dry or liquid | tsp. |
| tablespoon | dry or liquid | tbsp. |

# Liquid (Volume) Measurements

| Fluid Ounces | Tablespoons | Cups | Milliliter/ Liters | Pints | Quarts | Gallons |
|--------------|-------------|------|--------------------|-------|--------|---------|
| 1 fl oz | 2 tbsp. | $1/8$ cup | 30 ml | - | - | - |
| 2 fl oz | 4 tbsp. | ¼ cup | 60 ml | - | - | - |
| 4 fl oz | 8 tbsp. | ½ cup | 125 ml | - | - | |
| 8 fl oz | 16 tbsp. | 1 cup | 250 ml | - | - | - |
| 12 fl oz | - | 1 ½ cups | 375 ml | - | - | - |
| 16 fl oz | - | 2 cups | 500 ml | 1 pint | - | - |
| 32 fl oz | - | 4 cups | 1 L | 2 pints | 1 qt. | - |
| 128 fl oz | - | 16 cups | 4 L | 8 pints | 4 qts. | 1 gallon |

# THE FINISHING TOUCH

## Eric's Recipe Tips for Pressure Cooking

No matter what pressure cooker you're using, you need to always use AT LEAST one cup of liquid to cook your food. It doesn't really matter what that liquid is (water, broth, wine, etc), depending on the recipe. Because no liquid escapes the cooker in the form of steam, there is no "reduction" or evaporation. This is a good thing, because it keeps much of the flavor and nutrients intact. I like to use the least amount of liquid necessary for almost all recipes except for soups and stocks because it yields a more concentrated result. When I want a thicker result for my gravy, sauce or stew, there are many different ways to achieve that. Here are some of the ways I do this:

### ROUX

This is the most classic way to thicken sauces, soups, stews, etc. A roux is an equal mixture of wheat flour and fat (traditionally butter). The butter is melted in a small pot and then the flour is added. The mixture is stirred until the flour is well incorporated and the desired color has been achieved, about 2-3 minutes usually. The end result is a thickening agent to be added to your sauce, gravy or stew. If you use 1 oz. (2 tbsp.) of flour and 1 oz. (2 tbsp.) of butter, for instance, you could add that to a volume 8 times larger (in this case, 1 cup of your gravy or sauce) and it would be correctly proportioned as a thickening agent.

### SLURRY

Sometimes a slurry is preferable because you use half the amount of cornstarch to thicken that you would of flour. Also, it is gluten free and usually lump-free. To make a "slurry," mix one tablespoon of cornstarch with a ½ cup of cold water. Whisk until blended well and thickened. Add it to your sauce or gravy in the pressure cooker and, using the browning feature, bring it to a boil for just a few seconds, then hit the cxl/warm button to reduce the heat.

### INSTANT POTATO FLAKES

I don't remember how I found out about his trick, but I feel it is the easiest of all thickening methods. Simply add a ¼ cup of instant potato flakes to your sauce, gravy or stew and stir. After a couple of minutes, if you want an even thicker result, simply sprinkle in more flakes until desired thickness is achieved. This does not interfere with the flavor of your meal.

## SIMMERING

By simply utilizing the browning mode after you remove the lid from the pressure cooker, you can reduce your sauce or gravy using evaporation. If using the Power Pressure Cooker XL, remember that pushing any of the preset buttons will put you into browning mode as long as the lid is off.

## BUTTER

In a lot of cases, I like to add a tablespoon or two of butter (depending on the volume of the sauce/gravy) at the end of the cooking process. This adds a really nice shimmer and "mouth feel" to the sauce or gravy you've cooked.

## TOMATO PASTE

A staple that I use a lot in my dishes is tomato paste. If tomato is a flavor profile that you are adding to your dish, tomato paste is a great way to do that and it adds a thickness and richness to the final result. The paste will really shine through if you choose to reduce the sauce by simmering.

## DRIED HERBS

Just as in traditional cooking, you can use dried herbs during the cooking process but should not use them to "finish" the dish. In many cases, in the pressure cooker recipes you will use a lesser amount of dried herbs because no flavor is lost, and, in fact, flavors will be intensified during the pressure cooking process.

## FRESH HERBS

Wherever possible, I always recommend finishing the dishes you cook with chopped fresh herbs. This adds brightness and an extra layer of flavor at the end. Most of the time, fresh herbs won't stand up to pressure cooking (or any lengthy cooking for that matter). An exception to this would be what is referred to as a "bouquet garni," which is when you bundle fresh herbs, tie them together with twine and add it to the pot before cooking. An example of a typical bouquet would consist of parsley, basil, rosemary, bay leaf and thyme. This bouquet is removed prior to serving the food. Experiment with other herbs as you wish for stocks, soups and stews.

# SOUPS & STEWS

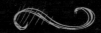

BEEF WITH SHALLOTS AND BARLEY

BEEF BRISKET STEW

BBQ PORK STEW WITH ORZO

TOSS AND GO BEEF STEW

QUICK CHICKEN STEW

CHICKEN NOODLE SOUP

TOSS AND GO CASSOULET

TURKEY POT PIE SOUP

TEX-MEX CHILI

SPLIT PEA SOUP WITH HAM

MEDITERRANEAN LAMB "CHILI"

ITALIAN WEDDING SOUP

CHICKEN TACO SOUP

CAPE COD CHOWDER

# BEEF WITH SHALLOTS AND BARLEY

## SERVES 4-6

## 1. TOSS IT!

Place all ingredients into desired cooker, tossing to combine.

## 2. COOK IT!

**Pressure Cooker**
Lock lid, close pressure valve, and set to HIGH for 20 minutes. Open pressure valve to quickly release the pressure.

**Slow Cooker**
Cover and set to LOW for 8 hours.

## 3. GO!

Serve immediately.

**ERIC'S TIP:** You can also substitute chunks of pork or veal in place of the beef.

## INGREDIENTS:

2 pounds beef chuck, cut into 1-inch cubes

5 cups beef stock

3 cups shallots, peeled and halved

1 cup pearl barley

½ cup diced carrot

½ cup diced celery

½ cup chopped sundried tomatoes

1 ounce dried porcini mushrooms

3 cloves garlic, chopped

¼ cup chopped fresh parsley

2 tablespoons chopped fresh thyme

2 tablespoons chopped fresh tarragon

2 teaspoons salt

2 teaspoons black pepper

1 teaspoon fennel seed

1 bay leaf

# BEEF BRISKET STEW

## SERVES 4-6

## 1. TOSS IT!

Place all ingredients, except peas and dried potato flakes, into desired cooker, tossing to combine.

## 2. COOK IT!

**Pressure Cooker**
Lock lid, close pressure valve, and set to HIGH for 45 minutes. Open pressure valve to quickly release the pressure.

**Slow Cooker**
Cover and set to LOW for 8 hours, or until beef is tender.

## 3. GO!

Stir in peas and dried potato flakes before serving.

**ERIC'S TIP:** You can also substitute chunks of pork or veal in place of the beef.

## INGREDIENTS:

3 to 4 pounds beef brisket, cut into 2-inch cubes

1 bag frozen pearl onions

1 cup chopped celery

1 cup chopped carrots

8 ounces sliced mushrooms

3 cups beef stock

3 tablespoons tomato paste

2 tablespoons Worcestershire sauce

2 teaspoons dried thyme

2 tablespoons beef stock concentrate, or two bouillon cubes crushed

3 tablespoons chopped garlic

3 teaspoons salt

2 teaspoons black pepper

1 cup frozen peas

½ cup dried potato flakes

# BBQ PORK STEW WITH ORZO

## SERVES 4–6

## 1. TOSS IT!

Place all ingredients, except orzo, butter, and parsley, into desired cooker, stirring to combine.

## 2. COOK IT!

**Pressure Cooker**
Lock lid, close pressure valve, and set to HIGH for 20 minutes. Open pressure valve to quickly release the pressure.

**Slow Cooker**
Cover and set to LOW for 6 hours.

## 3. GO!

Toss cooked orzo in butter and fresh parsley and serve smothered with the pork stew.

**ERIC'S TIP:** For a thicker stew, stir in ¼ cup of instant potato flakes after cooking.

## INGREDIENTS:

2 pounds pork shoulder, 1-inch cubed

4 cups beef stock

1 (14.5-ounce) can diced tomatoes

2 cups cremini mushrooms, sliced thick

1 cup diced onion

1 cup diced carrot

1 cup diced celery

¼ cup your favorite BBQ sauce

3 cloves garlic, chopped

2 tablespoons A-1 sauce

1 tablespoon tomato paste

1 tablespoon chopped fresh thyme

2 teaspoons salt

2 teaspoons black pepper

1 bay leaf

1 pound orzo pasta, cooked

3 tablespoons butter

3 tablespoons chopped fresh parsley

# TOSS AND GO BEEF STEW

## SERVES 4

## 1. TOSS IT!

Coat stew meat in flour before placing into desired cooker. Add all remaining ingredients, except potato flakes, tossing to combine.

## 2. COOK IT!

**Pressure Cooker**
Lock lid, close pressure valve, and set to HIGH for 15 minutes. Open pressure valve to quickly release the pressure.

**Slow Cooker**
Cover and set to LOW for 8 hours, or until beef is tender.

## 3. GO!

Stir in potato flakes to thicken the gravy before serving.

## INGREDIENTS:

1½ pounds beef stew meat

2 tablespoons all-purpose flour

2 cups beef stock

1 pound baby potatoes, halved

2 cups baby carrots

2 cups onion, large chop

1 cup celery, cut into 1-inch lengths

5 sprigs fresh thyme

1 bay leaf

2 tablespoons Worcestershire sauce

2 teaspoons minced garlic

1 teaspoon onion powder

1 teaspoon salt

1 teaspoon black pepper

½ cup instant mashed potato flakes

**ERIC'S TIP:** For a more robust flavor, use beef base (sold in jars in the broth/stock aisle) to make your beef stock, then add additional beef base (without water) to taste after cooking.

# QUICK CHICKEN STEW

## SERVES 4–6

### 1. TOSS IT!

Place all ingredients into desired cooker, tossing to combine.

### 2. COOK IT!

**Pressure Cooker**
Lock lid, close pressure valve, and set to HIGH for 40 minutes. Open pressure valve to quickly release the pressure.

**Slow Cooker**
Cover and set to LOW for 8–10 hours, until chicken is tender.

### 3. GO!

Serve immediately.

**ERIC'S TIP:** I like to experiment with other cuts of meat in this stew, especially short ribs or beef shank.

## INGREDIENTS:

3 pounds boneless, skinless chicken thighs, ½ inch cubed

1 (28-ounce) can crushed tomatoes

2 cups chicken stock

1 (10.5-ounce) can condensed cream of mushroom soup

1 cup onion, large chop

1 cup celery, large chop

1 cup carrot, large chop

8 ounces mushrooms, quartered

½ cup red wine

¼ cup tomato paste

3 tablespoons chopped garlic

2 tablespoons steak seasoning

1 tablespoon prepared horseradish

2 teaspoons dried thyme

# CHICKEN NOODLE SOUP

## SERVES 6

This classic recipe uses a frozen mix of vegetables (I like to use peas, carrots, and corn) to create the Chicken Noodle Soup you know and love, without a long shopping list and with a very minimal amount of prep.

## 1. TOSS IT!

**Pressure Cooker**
Place all ingredients into pressure cooker, stirring to combine.

**Slow Cooker**
Place chicken thighs, vegetables, thyme, vegetable oil, salt, pepper, and 1 cup of the chicken stock in slow cooker and stir to combine.

## 2. COOK IT!

**Pressure Cooker**
Lock lid, close pressure valve, and set to HIGH for 6 minutes. Open pressure valve to quickly release the pressure.

**Slow Cooker**
Cover and set to LOW for 4 hours. Boil the rotini pasta in the remaining chicken stock, until tender. Transfer cooked pasta and stock to the slow cooker, cover, and let cook an additional 15 minutes.

## 3. GO!

Remove any stalks of thyme before serving.

## INGREDIENTS:

1 pound boneless, skinless chicken thighs, chopped

12 ounces frozen mixed vegetables

6 sprigs fresh thyme

½ teaspoon dried turmeric

1 teaspoon tomato paste

1 tablespoon vegetable oil

1½ teaspoon salt

1 teaspoon black pepper

8 cups chicken stock

12 ounces rotini pasta

½ cup chopped fresh parsley

**ERIC'S TIP:** For even more flavor, add a bay leaf and a few stalks of diced celery to the pot before cooking.

# TOSS AND GO CASSOULET

## SERVES 6-8

A French casserole of beans and pork, cassoulet is the perfect dish to prepare in a pressure or slow cooker, as either cooker will really help to meld the flavors together.

## 1. TOSS IT!

**Pressure Cooker**

Place all ingredients, except salt, parsley, and mashed potato flakes into pressure cooker and toss to combine.

**Slow Cooker**

Cover beans with 2-inches of water and soak overnight. Drain and transfer to the slow cooker. Stir in all remaining ingredients, except salt, parsley, and potato flakes.

## 2. COOK IT!

**Pressure Cooker**

Lock lid, close pressure valve, and set to HIGH for 45 minutes. Let the pressure release naturally before opening lid.

**Slow Cooker**

Cover and set to LOW for 8 hours.

## 3. GO!

Season with the salt before serving. For a thicker broth, add instant mashed potato flakes, 2 tablespoons at a time, until thickened to your desired consistency.

**ERIC'S TIP:** It's best to season this with salt after cooking, as too much salt can inhibit the beans from cooking properly.

## INGREDIENTS:

1 pound dried Great Northern beans, rinsed

2 pounds boneless country style ribs

8 ounces pork belly or salt pork, chopped

5 cups chicken stock

¾ cup dry white wine

3 carrots, sliced

3 stalks celery, sliced

1 cup diced yellow onion

2 tablespoons tomato paste

1 tablespoon olive oil

1 tablespoon minced garlic

2 bay leaves

3 sprigs fresh thyme

3 sprigs fresh rosemary

½ tsp dried thyme

1¼ teaspoons black pepper

Salt

Fresh chopped parsley, for garnish

Instant mashed potato flakes, optional

# TURKEY POT PIE SOUP

## SERVES 4—6

With this recipe, you get all the goodness of a turkey pot pie, in a lighter, chowder-style soup that doesn't require rolling out any dough. Serve alongside buttery crackers to crumble on top.

## 1. TOSS IT!

Place all ingredients, except heavy cream, peas and potato flakes, into desired cooker, tossing to combine.

## 2. COOK IT!

**Pressure Cooker**
Lock lid, close pressure valve, and set to HIGH for 10 minutes. Open pressure valve to quickly release the pressure.

**Slow Cooker**
Cover and set to LOW for 4 hours.

## 3. GO!

Stir in heavy cream, peas and potato flakes to thicken soup before serving.

**ERIC'S TIP:** This can also be made with chopped boneless chicken thighs if fresh (non-marinated) turkey tenderloin isn't available at your local grocery store.

## INGREDIENTS:

1 pound turkey tenderloin, chopped

5 cups chicken stock

4 carrots, sliced

3 stalks celery, diced

1 cup diced yellow onion

3 sprigs fresh thyme

2 tablespoons butter

1 teaspoon salt

1 teaspoon black pepper

¾ cup heavy cream

1 cup frozen peas

1½ cups instant mashed potato flakes

# TEX-MEX CHILI

## SERVES 4—6

This colorful chili is bursting with peppers, onions, corn, and black beans. For the perfect presentation, stir a handful of chopped cilantro and a splash of lime juice into sour cream, topping each bowl with a dollop.

## 1. TOSS IT!

Place ground beef into desired cooker, breaking into small pieces. Add all remaining ingredients, except black beans, stirring to combine.

## 2. COOK IT!

**Pressure Cooker**
Lock lid, close pressure valve, and set to HIGH for 6 minutes. Open pressure valve to quickly release the pressure.

**Slow Cooker**
Cover and set to LOW for 6 hours.

## 3. GO!

Stir in black beans before serving.

### INGREDIENTS:

1 pound lean ground beef

2 (14.5-ounce) cans diced tomatoes, with liquid

2 bell peppers (any color), chopped

1 cup frozen corn kernels

1 red onion, diced

2 jalapeño peppers, seeded and diced

¼ cup chopped cilantro

3 tablespoons tomato paste

1 tablespoon light brown sugar

1 tablespoon chili powder

2 teaspoons salt

1½ teaspoons black pepper

1 teaspoon paprika

1 teaspoon cumin

1 teaspoon coriander

1 (15-ounce) can black beans, drained

# SPLIT PEA SOUP WITH HAM

## SERVES 6-8

Whether you are slow cooking or preparing under pressure, there's no need to pre-soak the peas in this classic soup. Simply toss and go! For the least amount of work, use diced ham in place of a ham hock and there will be no need to shred the ham and remove the bone after cooking.

## 1. TOSS IT!

Place all ingredients into desired cooker, stirring to combine.

## 2. COOK IT!

**Pressure Cooker**
Lock lid, close pressure valve, and set to HIGH for 15 minutes. Open pressure valve to quickly release the pressure.

**Slow Cooker**
Cover and set to LOW for 8–10 hours, until peas are tender.

## 3. GO!

Remove bay leaves, and if using ham hocks or shanks, shred the meat and remove the bones before serving. Add the butter and potato flakes stir to combine.

### INGREDIENTS:

1 pound green split peas, rinsed

1 smoked ham hock, or 1 pound ham shanks or diced ham

6½ cups chicken stock or broth

2 carrots, sliced or chopped

2 stalks celery, diced

1 yellow onion, diced

1 tablespoon olive oil

2 bay leaves

2 teaspoons minced garlic

1 teaspoon dried thyme

¾ teaspoon salt

¾ teaspoon black pepper

½ cup potato flakes

2 tablespoons butter

**ERIC'S TIP:** The soup will thicken if rested for 5 minutes. If it is too thick for your liking, thin it out with chicken stock or water. If it is too thin, you can thicken it further with instant potato flakes, adding just 1 tablespoon at a time, until you've reached your desired consistency.

# MEDITERRANEAN LAMB "CHILI"

## SERVES 6

## 1. TOSS IT!

Place all ingredients, except Greek yogurt, fresh herbs, and lemon zest, into desired cooker, tossing to combine.

## 2. COOK IT!

**Pressure Cooker**
Lock lid, close pressure valve, and set to HIGH for 15 minutes. Open pressure valve to quickly release the pressure.

**Slow Cooker**
Cover and set to LOW for 6 hours.

## 3. GO!

Stir in yogurt, fresh herbs, and lemon zest before serving.

**ERIC'S TIP:** If you want to take your Greek yogurt up to the next level, check your market for Skyr. It's Icelandic yogurt that is twice as thick as its Greek counterpart.

### INGREDIENTS:

2 pounds ground lamb, broken up

3 cups beef stock

1 (15-ounce) can garbanzo beans, drained and rinsed

1 (15-ounce) can white beans, drained and rinsed

1 (14.5-ounce) can diced tomatoes, with liquid

8 ounces cremini mushrooms, sliced

1 red bell pepper, chopped

½ cup chopped onion

½ cup chopped carrot

½ cup chopped celery

½ cup chopped sundried tomatoes

2 tablespoons chopped garlic

1 teaspoon salt

1 teaspoon black pepper

½ teaspoon allspice

½ teaspoon cardamom

1 cup plain Greek yogurt

¼ cup chopped fresh parsley

3 tablespoons chopped fresh oregano

1 tablespoon chopped fresh thyme

Zest of one lemon

# ITALIAN WEDDING SOUP

## SERVES 4—6

## 1. TOSS IT!

Place all ingredients except cheese and basil, into desired cooker, tossing to combine.

## 2. COOK IT!

### Pressure Cooker
Lock lid, close pressure valve, and set to HIGH for 7 minutes. Open pressure valve to quickly release the pressure.

### Slow Cooker
Cover and set to LOW for 4 hours.

## 3. GO!

Stir in the cheese and basil before serving.

**ERIC'S TIP:** I also love this soup with leftover rice added after the cooking process in place of the orzo.

## INGREDIENTS:

1 pound hot Italian sausage, removed from casings and rolled into ½-inch balls

7 cups chicken stock

1 (1-pound) bag frozen chopped spinach

1 cup diced onion

½ cup sundried tomato, chopped

1 cup diced carrots

1 cup diced celery

3 cloves garlic, chopped

2 teaspoons salt

2 teaspoons black pepper

8 ounces orzo pasta

¼ cup chopped fresh basil

1 cup grated Parmesan cheese

# CHICKEN TACO SOUP

## SERVES 4–6

## 1. TOSS IT!

Place all ingredients, except tortillas and cilantro, into desired cooker, tossing to combine.

## 2. COOK IT!

### Pressure Cooker
Lock lid, close pressure valve, and set to HIGH for 15 minutes. Open pressure valve to quickly release the pressure.

### Slow Cooker
Cover and set to LOW for 6 hours.

## 3. GO!

Stir in corn tortillas and cilantro before serving.

**ERIC'S TIP:** I like to top this with a drizzle of fresh lime juice and a dollop of sour cream that melts right into the broth.

## INGREDIENTS:

2 pounds boneless, skinless chicken thighs, chopped into 1-inch pieces

5 cups chicken stock

1 (15-ounce) can black beans, drained and rinsed

1 (14.5-ounce) can diced tomatoes

2 cups chopped red onion

2 cups chopped green bell pepper

1 cup diced celery

1 (4-ounce) can green chiles

3 cloves garlic, chopped

1 tablespoon chopped chipotle pepper

2 tablespoons cumin

2 tablespoons paprika

2 teaspoons salt

2 teaspoons black pepper

2 cups chopped corn tortillas

¼ cup chopped fresh cilantro

# CAPE COD CHOWDER

## SERVES 4–6

This taste of New England substitutes flakes of tender cod for the clams you'd traditionally find in a white chowder. Thickening the soup with instant mashed potato flakes not only makes this much easier than thickening with flour, but adds all the flavor of chopped potatoes, without having to actually chop any potatoes!

## 1. TOSS IT!

Place all ingredients, except heavy cream, potato flakes, and parsley, into desired cooker, tossing to combine.

## 2. COOK IT!

**Pressure Cooker**
Lock lid, close pressure valve, and set to HIGH for 4 minutes. Open pressure valve to quickly release the pressure.

**Slow Cooker**
Cover and set to LOW for 3 hours.

## 3. GO!

Break up fish fillets into the broth, then stir in heavy cream and potato flakes to thicken. Serve garnished with fresh parsley.

**ERIC'S TIP:** The clam juice in this recipe adds more seafood flavor, however, additional water can be substituted to let the mild flavor of the cod shine.

## INGREDIENTS:

2 frozen cod fillets

2 cups frozen corn kernels

8 strips precooked bacon, diced

1 cup clam juice

2¾ cups water

1 cup diced yellow onion

½ cup diced red bell pepper

2 sprigs fresh thyme

2 tablespoons butter

1/2 teaspoon ground thyme

1 bay leaf

1 teaspoon salt

1 teaspoon black pepper

1 cup heavy cream

1½ cups instant mashed potato flakes

Chopped fresh parsley, for garnish

# PASTA, RICE & RISOTTO

CHEDDAR AND CHORIZO PASTA

HAM 'N CHEESE MAC AND CHEESE

CREAMY ZITI WITH MEATBALLS

HAM AND MUSSEL RISOTTO

HAWAIIAN HAM "FRIED" RICE

PASTA FRA DIAVOLO

JALAPEÑO MAC AND CHEESE

PASTA WITH CLAMS

PESTO CHICKEN RISOTTO

TURKEY PEPPERONI RIGATONI

CLASSIC MAC AND CHEESE

SMOKY BACON AND GOUDA GRITS

SUMMER SUCCOTASH RISOTTO

SUPER EASY PENNE A LA VODKA

TUNA, PEA, AND MUSHROOM ROTINI

BOLOGNESE SAUCE

# CHEDDAR AND CHORIZO PASTA

## SERVES 6

## 1. TOSS IT!

**Pressure Cooker**
Add cheese soup and 2 cans of water to the pressure cooker and stir in all remaining ingredients, except Parmesan cheese. Add any additional water as necessary to ensure all pasta is submerged.

**Slow Cooker**
Boil the penne pasta for ¾ the time recommended on the package. Drain, transfer to the slow cooker. Add cheese soup and 1 can of water to the slow cooker and stir in all remaining ingredients, except Parmesan cheese.

## 2. COOK IT!

**Pressure Cooker**
Lock lid, close pressure valve, and set to HIGH for 5 minutes. Open pressure valve to quickly release the pressure.

**Slow Cooker**
Cover and set to LOW for 1 hour.

## 3. GO!

Stir in Parmesan cheese and season with salt and pepper to taste before serving.

**ERIC'S TIP:** This is even better when topped with fresh chopped cilantro before serving.

## INGREDIENTS:

2 (10.75-ounce) cans condensed cheddar cheese soup (no water added)

1 pound penne pasta

1 pound fully cooked chorizo, thinly sliced

2 cups diced fresh tomatoes

2 cups onion, chopped

1 cup half and half

1 (4.5-ounce) can chopped green chilies

2 tablespoons butter

1 teaspoon dried cilantro leaves

½ cup grated Parmesan cheese

Salt and black pepper, to taste

# HAM 'N CHEESE MAC AND CHEESE

## SERVES 6

## 1. TOSS IT!

**Pressure Cooker**
Add 4 cups of water to the pressure cooker and stir in elbow macaroni, vegetable oil, ham, onion powder, and garlic powder.

**Slow Cooker**
Boil the elbow macaroni for ¾ the time recommended on the package. Drain, transfer to the slow cooker, and stir in all remaining ingredients, plus ½ cup water.

## 2. COOK IT!

**Pressure Cooker**
Lock lid, close pressure valve, and set to HIGH for 5 minutes. Open pressure valve to quickly release the pressure. Remove lid and stir in all remaining ingredients.

**Slow Cooker**
Cover and set to LOW for 1 hour.

## 3. GO!

Stir to fully incorporate the cheese into the sauce before seasoning with salt and pepper to taste.

## INGREDIENTS:

1 pound elbow macaroni

1 tablespoon vegetable oil

8 ounces cubed ham

½ teaspoon onion powder

½ teaspoon garlic powder

8 ounces shredded Swiss cheese

8 ounces shredded cheddar cheese

1 cup grated Parmesan cheese

¾ cup milk

4 ounces sour cream

4 ounces cream cheese

Salt and pepper

**ERIC'S TIP:** When pressure cooking, set your cooker to warm to help melt the cheeses as you stir them in.

# CREAMY ZITI WITH MEATBALLS

## SERVES 6

## 1. TOSS IT!

### Pressure Cooker

Add 4 cups of water to the cooker. Stir in spaghetti sauce, pasta, oil, salt, and pepper, ensuring pasta is fully submerged under the liquid. Top with the frozen meatballs.

### Slow Cooker

Place meatballs, spaghetti sauce, oil, salt, and pepper in cooker and stir to coat meatballs.

## 2. COOK IT!

### Pressure Cooker

Lock lid, close pressure valve, and set to HIGH for 5 minutes. Open pressure valve to quickly release the pressure. Remove lid and stir in ricotta and Parmesan cheese.

### Slow Cooker

Cover and set to LOW for 4 hours. Boil the ziti pasta for ¾ of the time recommended on the package. Drain and transfer cooked ziti to the slow cooker and stir in ricotta and Parmesan cheeses. Cover and cook an additional 30 minutes.

## 3. GO!

Serve garnished with chopped fresh parsley.

## INGREDIENTS:

1 (24-28 ounces) bag frozen meatballs

1 (24-ounce) jar prepared spaghetti sauce

1 pound ziti pasta

1 tablespoon vegetable oil

1 teaspoon salt

½ teaspoon black pepper

1 cup part-skim ricotta cheese

½ cup grated Parmesan cheese

Chopped fresh parsley, for garnish

**ERIC'S TIP:** For more flavor, 2 teaspoons of dried or 2 tablespoons of fresh Italian herbs can be added before cooking. I also like to stir in a splash of balsamic vinegar after cooking to let the acid wake up the flavors.

# HAM AND MUSSEL RISOTTO

## SERVES 6—8

## 1. TOSS IT!

Place rice and olive oil into desired cooker and toss to combine. Stir in all remaining ingredients, except mussels, Parmesan cheese, and parsley.

## 2. COOK IT!

**Pressure Cooker**
Lock lid, close pressure valve, and set to HIGH for 8 minutes. Open pressure valve to quickly release the pressure.

**Slow Cooker**
Cover and set to HIGH for 1 hour. Stir and top with mussels before covering to cook an additional 30 minutes, just until rice is tender and mussels have opened.

## 3. GO!

Discard any mussels that did not open. Season with salt and pepper to taste and serve topped with Parmesan cheese and parsley.

**ERIC'S TIP:** This works well as an appetizer or dinner. Risotto will thicken as it cools, but can be thinned out with additional water or stock.

## INGREDIENTS:

2 cups Arborio Rice

3 tablespoons olive oil

2 (16-ounce) cans Italian-style white clam sauce

8 ounces diced ham

½ cup white wine (I use sauvignon blanc)

½ cup sherry wine

¼ cup chopped sundried tomatoes

Zest and juice of one lemon

2 tablespoons Dijon mustard

2 pounds mussels (about 50)

Salt and black pepper to taste

½ cup Parmesan cheese

½ cup chopped parsley

# HAWAIIAN HAM "FRIED" RICE

## SERVES 4

## 1. TOSS IT!

Place all ingredients, except pineapple and green onions, into desired cooker and toss to combine.

## 2. COOK IT!

**Pressure Cooker**
Lock lid, close pressure valve, and set to HIGH for 6 minutes. Open pressure valve to quickly release the pressure.

**Slow Cooker**
Cover and set to HIGH for 2 hours, or until rice is tender.

## 3. GO!

Stir in pineapple and green onions before serving.

**ERIC'S TIP:** 3 tablespoons of regular soy sauce and 1 tablespoon of additional water can be used in place of the reduced-sodium soy sauce.

## INGREDIENTS:

1½ cups long grain white rice, rinsed

2¼ cups water

12 ounces cubed ham

½ cup diced red bell pepper

¼ cup reduced-sodium soy sauce

2 teaspoons sesame oil

2 teaspoons light brown sugar

1 teaspoon minced garlic

1 (20-ounce) can pineapple chunks, drained

½ cup sliced green onions

# PASTA FRA DIAVOLO

## SERVES 4—6

## 1. TOSS IT!

**Pressure Cooker**

Add 2 cups of water to the pressure cooker and stir in all remaining ingredients, except marinara sauce and basil. Add any additional water as necessary to ensure all pasta is submerged.

**Slow Cooker**

Boil the gemelli pasta for ¾ the time recommended on the package. Drain, transfer to the slow cooker, and stir in all remaining ingredients, except marinara sauce and basil.

## 2. COOK IT!

**Pressure Cooker**

Lock lid, close pressure valve, and set to HIGH for 5 minutes. Open pressure valve to quickly release the pressure.

**Slow Cooker**

Cover and set to LOW for 1 hour.

## 3. GO!

Stir in marinara sauce and basil before serving.

## INGREDIENTS:

1 pound gemelli pasta

1 (14-5) ounce can crushed tomatoes

½ cup chopped roasted red peppers

1 tablespoon capers

1 tablespoon chopped garlic

½ teaspoon dried oregano

1 tablespoon balsamic vinegar

1 teaspoon salt

1 teaspoon black pepper

½-1 teaspoon red pepper flakes

½ cup prepared marinara sauce

¼ cup chopped fresh basil

# JALAPEÑO MAC AND CHEESE

## SERVES 6

This simple and comforting white cheddar macaroni and cheese is inspired by cream cheese filled jalapeño poppers. Fresh jalapeño adds just a bit of spice (they cook up more mildly than you'd think) and crushed croutons make a perfect topping to both replicate baked mac and cheese, as well as the breading on a jalapeño popper.

## 1. TOSS IT!

### Pressure Cooker
Add 5 cups of water to the pressure cooker and stir in elbow macaroni, vegetable oil, salt, and pepper.

### Slow Cooker
Boil the elbow macaroni for ¾ the time recommended on the package. Drain, transfer to the slow cooker, and stir in all remaining ingredients, except croutons. Add 1½ cups of water.

## 2. COOK IT!

### Pressure Cooker
Lock lid, close pressure valve, and set to HIGH for 5 minutes. Open pressure valve to quickly release the pressure. Remove lid and stir in cheddar and cream cheese.

### Slow Cooker
Cover and set to LOW for 1 hour.

## 3. GO!

Stir to fully incorporate the cheese into the sauce before serving topped with crushed croutons.

## INGREDIENTS:

1 pound elbow macaroni

4 large jalapeño peppers, seeded and diced

1 tablespoon vegetable oil

1½ teaspoons salt

½ teaspoon black pepper

8 ounces shredded sharp white cheddar cheese

4 ounces cream cheese, cubed

1 cup crushed croutons

**ERIC'S TIP:** It should go without saying, but yellow sharp cheddar cheese can be used in place of the white, as it is far easier to find pre-shredded, saving on prep-time.

# PASTA WITH CLAMS

## SERVES 4–6

## 1. TOSS IT!

**Pressure Cooker**

Add 2 cups of water to the pressure cooker and stir in all remaining ingredients, except prepared sauce and parsley. Add any additional water as necessary to ensure all pasta is submerged.

**Slow Cooker**

Boil the cavatappi pasta for ¾ the time recommended on the package. Drain, transfer to the slow cooker, and stir in all remaining ingredients, except prepared sauce and parsley.

## 2. COOK IT!

**Pressure Cooker**

Lock lid, close pressure valve, and set to HIGH for 5 minutes. Open pressure valve to quickly release the pressure.

**Slow Cooker**

Cover and set to LOW for 1 hour.

## 3. GO!

Stir in your choice of prepared sauce before serving, topped with chopped parsley.

**ERIC'S TIP:** For the most tender clams, drain the liquid from the cans of clams into the cooker before cooking, but stir the actual clams (they're fully cooked) in after cooking.

### INGREDIENTS:

1 pound cavatappi pasta

1 (10-ounce) can whole clams in juice

1 (6-ounce) can chopped clams in juice

1 cup of clam juice

¼ cup dry white wine

2 tablespoons chopped garlic

1 teaspoon dried thyme

1 teaspoon salt

1 teaspoon black pepper

¼ teaspoon crushed red pepper flakes

1 cup prepared marinara or Alfredo sauce

¼ cup chopped fresh parsley

# PESTO CHICKEN RISOTTO

## SERVES 6

By using prepared pesto sauce that you can buy in a jar (in the pasta aisle) or a refrigerated container (near the fresh pasta in the grocery store), I've cut a considerable amount of prep-time from this taste of Italy. For a complete meal, simply add frozen broccoli florets before cooking.

## 1. TOSS IT!

Place rice and olive oil into desired cooker and toss to combine. Stir in all remaining ingredients, except Parmesan cheese.

## 2. COOK IT!

**Pressure Cooker**
Lock lid, close pressure valve, and set to HIGH for 6 minutes. Open pressure valve to quickly release the pressure.

**Slow Cooker**
Cover and set to HIGH for 1½ hours, just until rice is tender and chicken is cooked through. For best results, stir halfway through cooking.

## 3. GO!

Stir in Parmesan cheese before serving.

### INGREDIENTS:

2 cups Arborio rice

1 tablespoon olive oil

2 boneless, skinless chicken breasts, chopped

5 cups chicken stock or broth

1 cup diced yellow onion

¾ cup prepared pesto sauce

Juice of ½ lemon

1 teaspoon black pepper

½ teaspoon salt

½ cup grated Parmesan cheese

**ERIC'S TIP:** Risotto will thicken as it cools, but can be thinned out with additional chicken stock or water.

# TURKEY PEPPERONI RIGATONI

## SERVES 6–8

## 1. TOSS IT!

**Pressure Cooker**
Add 3 cups of water to the pressure cooker and stir in all remaining ingredients, except Parmesan cheese. Add any additional water as necessary to ensure all pasta is submerged.

**Slow Cooker**
Boil the rigatoni pasta for ¾ the time recommended on the package. Drain, transfer to the slow cooker, and stir in all remaining ingredients, except Parmesan cheese.

## 2. COOK IT!

**Pressure Cooker**
Lock lid, close pressure valve, and set to HIGH for 5 minutes. Open pressure valve to quickly release the pressure.

**Slow Cooker**
Cover and set to LOW for 1 hour.

## 3. GO!

Stir in Parmesan cheese before serving.

### INGREDIENTS:

1 pound rigatoni pasta

1 (14.5-ounce) can diced tomatoes, with liquid

8 ounces turkey pepperoni, chopped

8 ounces sliced mushrooms

¼ cup chopped sundried tomatoes

¼ cup prepared pesto sauce

1 tablespoon chopped garlic

1 teaspoon salt

1 teaspoon black pepper

¼ cup grated Parmesan cheese

**ERIC'S TIP:** For even more flavor, substitute chicken stock for the water added to the pressure cooker, or the water used to boil the pasta before slow cooking.

# CLASSIC MAC AND CHEESE

## SERVES 6

## 1. TOSS IT!

**Pressure Cooker**
Add 4 cups of water to the pressure cooker and stir in elbow macaroni, garlic powder, salt, and pepper.

**Slow Cooker**
Boil the elbow macaroni for ¾ the time recommended on the package. Drain, transfer to the slow cooker, and stir in all remaining ingredients.

## 2. COOK IT!

**Pressure Cooker**
Lock lid, close pressure valve, and set to HIGH for 5 minutes. Open pressure valve to quickly release the pressure. Remove lid and stir in cheeses, milk, and nutmeg.

**Slow Cooker**
Cover and set to LOW for 1 hour.

## 3. GO!

Stir to fully incorporate the cheese into the sauce before serving.

**ERIC'S TIP:** For that homestyle feel, serve topped with crumbled croutons.

## INGREDIENTS:

1 pound elbow macaroni

1 teaspoon garlic powder

1 1/2 teaspoons salt

1 teaspoon black pepper

3 cups shredded sharp cheddar cheese

¼ cup grated Romano cheese

4 ounces Velveeta cheese, cubed

2 cups milk

¼ teaspoon ground nutmeg

# SMOKY BACON AND GOUDA GRITS

## SERVES 4–6

I find that grits labeled "old fashioned," not instant or "quick cooking," have a far better flavor and texture than the latter, while also being able to hold up to slow or pressure cooking.

## 1. TOSS IT!

Place all ingredients, except gouda cheese and green onions, into desired cooker and stir to combine.

## 2. COOK IT!

**Pressure Cooker**
Lock lid, close pressure valve, and set to HIGH for 6 minutes. Open pressure valve to quickly release the pressure.

**Slow Cooker**
Cover and set to LOW for 3 hours.

## 3. GO!

Stir in gouda cheese and green onions before serving.

**ERIC'S TIP:** For classic cheese grits, bacon and green onions can be omitted and gouda can be replaced with 1 cup of shredded sharp cheddar cheese.

### INGREDIENTS:

1 cup old fashioned grits

3 cups water

1 cup whole milk

8 strips precooked bacon, chopped

2 tablespoons butter

1 teaspoon salt

¾ teaspoon pepper

4 ounces smoked gouda, shredded or diced

½ cup sliced green onions

# SUMMER SUCCOTASH RISOTTO

## SERVES 6

This colorful risotto may seem complicated but can be made using only a few pantry ingredients and without standing by the stove to stir. Frozen mixed vegetables help cut down on prep-work, while ensuring that the vegetables finish cooking at the same time as the rice.

## 1. TOSS IT!

Place rice and olive oil into desired cooker and toss to combine. Stir in all remaining ingredients, except Parmesan and parsley.

## 2. COOK IT!

**Pressure Cooker**
Lock lid, close pressure valve, and set to HIGH for 6 minutes. Open pressure valve to quickly release the pressure.

**Slow Cooker**
Cover and set to HIGH for 1½ hours, just until rice is tender. For best results, stir halfway through cooking.

## 3. GO!

Remove bay leaf and stir in Parmesan cheese before serving, topped with chopped parsley.

**ERIC'S TIP:** Risotto will thicken as it cools, but can be thinned out with additional chicken stock or water.

### INGREDIENTS:

2 cups chicken stock

2 cups Arborio rice

1 tablespoon olive oil

5 cups vegetable stock or broth

2½ cups frozen succotash (mixed) vegetables

¾ cup white wine

1 cup diced red onion

1 teaspoon minced garlic

1 teaspoon black pepper

¾ teaspoon salt

1 bay leaf

1 cup grated Parmesan cheese

Chopped fresh parsley

# SUPER EASY PENNE A LA VODKA

## SERVES 4–6

## 1. TOSS IT!

### Pressure Cooker
Add 3 cups of water to the pressure cooker and stir in all remaining ingredients, except cream cheese and basil. Add any additional water as necessary to ensure all pasta is submerged.

### Slow Cooker
Boil the penne pasta for ¾ the time recommended on the package. Drain, transfer to the slow cooker, and stir in all remaining ingredients, except basil.

## 2. COOK IT!

### Pressure Cooker
Lock lid, close pressure valve, and set to HIGH for 5 minutes. Open pressure valve to quickly release the pressure. Stir in cream cheese.

### Slow Cooker
Cover and set to LOW for 1 hour.

## 3. GO!

Serve topped with chopped fresh basil.

## INGREDIENTS:

1 pound penne pasta

1 (14.5-ounce) can diced tomatoes, with liquid

1 cup prepared marinara sauce

8 ounces sliced mushrooms

3 tablespoons vodka

1 tablespoon chopped sundried tomatoes

1 tablespoon chopped garlic

1 teaspoon salt

1 teaspoon black pepper

4 ounces cream cheese, softened

3 tablespoons chopped fresh basil

**ERIC'S TIP:** The alcohol in the vodka may not cook out when slow-cooking. To ensure that it does, you can bring the marinara sauce and vodka to a simmer for 2 minutes before adding to the slow cooker. You can also omit the vodka entirely for either preparation, however alcohol brings out certain flavor compounds in tomatoes that really make this dish delicious.

# TUNA, PEA, AND MUSHROOM ROTINI

## SERVES 6—8

## 1. TOSS IT!

**Pressure Cooker**
Place all ingredients, except peas and Parmesan cheese in the pressure cooker, stirring to combine.

**Slow Cooker**
Bring the vegetable stock to a boil and add rotini, boiling until ¾ of the stock is absorbed by the pasta, about 6 minutes. Transfer pasta and stock to the slow cooker and stir in all remaining ingredients.

## 2. COOK IT!

**Pressure Cooker**
Lock lid, close pressure valve, and set to HIGH for 5 minutes. Open pressure valve to quickly release the pressure. Remove lid and stir in peas and Parmesan cheese.

**Slow Cooker**
Cover and set to LOW for 1 hour, or until bubbly hot.

## 3. GO!

Serve topped with additional Parmesan cheese, if desired.

### INGREDIENTS:

5 cups vegetable stock

1½ pounds dry rotini pasta

2 (10.5-ounce) cans cream of mushroom soup

3 (5-ounce) cans tuna, drained

1 pound sliced mushrooms

1½ cups frozen chopped onions

2 (4-ounce) jars sliced pimentos, drained

1¼ cup sherry cooking wine

½ teaspoon dried thyme

¼ teaspoon garlic powder

½ teaspoons salt

½ teaspoon black pepper

2 cups frozen peas

1 cup grated Parmesan cheese

# BOLOGNESE SAUCE

## SERVES 4–6

## 1. TOSS IT!

Place all ingredients, except basil and milk, into desired cooker, breaking up the ground beef as you toss together.

## 2. COOK IT!

**Pressure Cooker**
Lock lid, close pressure valve, and set to HIGH for 25 minutes. Open pressure valve to quickly release the pressure.

**Slow Cooker**
Cover and set to LOW for 6 hours.

## 3. GO!

Stir in basil, milk, and grated cheese before serving over cooked pasta.

**ERIC'S TIP:** Ground chicken, turkey, or even spicy sausage (removed from their casings) can be used in place of the ground beef. I highly recommend a mix of pork, beef, and veal commonly used in meatloaf.

## INGREDIENTS:

2 pounds very lean ground beef

1 cup minced onion

1 cup minced celery

1 cup minced carrots

8 ounces mushrooms, sliced

1 (6-ounce) can tomato paste

1 (28-ounce) can crushed tomatoes

⅓ cup sundried tomatoes, chopped

3 tablespoons chopped garlic

2 teaspoons salt

3 teaspoons black pepper

1 teaspoon dried basil

½ cup fresh basil, chopped

½ cup milk

½ cup grated Romano cheese

# POULTRY

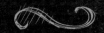

SWEET AND SAVORY TURKEY BREAST

RED CURRY CHICKEN

HONEY GARLIC CHICKEN WITH VEGETABLES

QUINOA WITH CHICKEN SAUSAGE AND KALE

ORCHARD GLAZED WINGS

MOROCCAN WINGS

MISO AND SOY GLAZED CHICKEN

GREEK CHICKEN AND RICE

CHICKEN TIKKA MASALA

COQ AU VIN (EASY CHICKEN STEW)

CHICKEN SAUSAGE WITH FENNEL

CHICKEN CASSOULET

CHICKEN CARBONARA PASTA

CHICKEN AND RICE VERDE

CHICKEN AND BACON WITH WILD RICE

BOURBON CHICKEN AND BROCCOLI

CHICKEN AND ARTICHOKE PICCATA

BONELESS CHICKEN CACCIATORE

# SWEET AND SAVORY TURKEY BREAST

## SERVES 6

## 1. TOSS IT!

Place all ingredients, except turkey, potato flakes, and butter, into desired cooker, tossing to combine. Top with the turkey breast and baste with sauce from the cooker.

## 2. COOK IT!

**Pressure Cooker**
Lock lid, close pressure valve, and set to HIGH for 25 minutes. Open pressure valve to quickly release the pressure.

**Slow Cooker**
Cover and set to HIGH for 1 hour. Switch cooker to LOW and continue cooking for an additional 6 hours.

## 3. GO!

Set turkey on a serving platter and let rest 10 minutes before carving. Meanwhile, stir potato flakes and butter into the gravy in the cooker, to thicken.

**ERIC'S TIP:** For an even richer gravy, add ¼ cup of heavy cream when you are stirring in the instant potato flakes.

## INGREDIENTS:

2 (10.5-ounce) cans condensed French onion soup (no water added)

1 (14-ounce) can jellied cranberry sauce

2 onions, chopped

2 stalks celery, chopped

2 carrots, chopped

1 cup water

1 tablespoon apple cider vinegar

1 teaspoon dried thyme

1 teaspoon dried tarragon

1 teaspoon paprika

1 (5-pound) bone-in turkey breast

½ cup instant mashed potato flakes

1 tablespoon butter

# RED CURRY CHICKEN

## SERVES 4–6

## 1. TOSS IT!

Place all ingredients, except scallions, basil, and mint, into desired cooker, tossing to combine.

## 2. COOK IT!

### Pressure Cooker
Lock lid, close pressure valve, and set to HIGH for 15 minutes. Open pressure valve to quickly release the pressure.

### Slow Cooker
Cover and set to LOW for 4 hours, or until chicken is cooked throughout.

## 3. GO!

Stir in scallions, basil, and mint before serving.

**ERIC'S TIP:** Lemongrass paste is sold in small tubes in a refrigerated case in the produce section (next to the small packages of fresh herbs).

### INGREDIENTS:

2–3 pounds boneless, skinless chicken breasts

1 (14-ounce) can unsweetened coconut milk

1 cup chopped onion

1 cup chopped green bell pepper

1 cup chopped red bell pepper

1 cup sliced mushrooms

3 cloves garlic, chopped

3 tablespoons red curry paste

3 tablespoons grated fresh ginger

1 tablespoon lemongrass paste (see tip)

½ cup chopped scallions

¼ cup chopped fresh basil

1 tablespoon chopped fresh mint

# HONEY GARLIC CHICKEN WITH VEGETABLES

## SERVES 4

## 1. TOSS IT!

Place all ingredients, except cornstarch mixture, scallions, and sesame seeds, into desired cooker, tossing to combine.

## 2. COOK IT!

**Pressure Cooker**
Lock lid, close pressure valve, and set to HIGH for 3 minutes. Open pressure valve to quickly release the pressure.

**Slow Cooker**
Cover and set to LOW for 4 hours.

## 3. GO!

To thicken the sauce, bring up to a simmer (either within your cooker or on the stove for traditional slow cookers). Whisk the cornstarch mixture into the simmering sauce and let cook 2 minutes, until thickened. Serve garnished with scallions and toasted sesame seeds.

**ERIC'S TIP:** Like most Asian recipes, this is perfect when served over white rice. I like to buy the pre-cooked microwave pouches for the least amount of added work.

### INGREDIENTS:

2 pounds boneless, skinless chicken breasts, sliced into ½-inch strips

1 (20-ounce) bag frozen Asian vegetable medley, thawed

½ cup soy sauce

⅓ cup honey

¼ cup ketchup

¼ cup rice wine vinegar

¼ cup chicken stock or water

2 teaspoons minced garlic

2 teaspoons minced ginger

2 teaspoons sesame oil

2 tablespoons cornstarch whisked into 3 tablespoons cold water

2 scallions, sliced

1 teaspoon toasted sesame seeds

# QUINOA WITH CHICKEN SAUSAGE AND KALE

## SERVES 4

This light and wholesome dinner is made with protein-packed quinoa, antioxidant-rich kale, and flavorful red bell pepper, which actually has more vitamin C than an orange! Low-fat chicken sausage completes the meal.

## 1. TOSS IT!

Place all ingredients into desired cooker except the cheese, tossing to combine.

## 2. COOK IT!

**Pressure Cooker**
Lock lid, close pressure valve, and set to HIGH for 3 minutes. Open pressure valve to quickly release the pressure.

**Slow Cooker**
Cover and set to LOW for 4 hours. For best results, stir halfway through cooking.

## 3. GO!

Let rest with the lid off for 3 minutes before fluffing with a fork. Add the feta cheese and serve.

**ERIC'S TIP:** For a nice presentation, I like to use tri-color quinoa in this recipe.

### INGREDIENTS:

1½ cups quinoa

1 (12-ounce) package fully-cooked chicken sausage, sliced thick

3½ cups chicken stock

2 cups frozen chopped kale

1 red bell pepper, diced

½ teaspoon dried oregano

1 teaspoon onion powder

1 teaspoon chili powder

1 tablespoon chopped garlic

½ teaspoon salt

½ teaspoon black pepper

½ cup crumbled feta cheese

# ORCHARD GLAZED WINGS

## SERVES 4—6

## 1. TOSS IT!

Place all ingredients into desired cooker, tossing to combine.

## 2. COOK IT!

**Pressure Cooker**
Lock lid, close pressure valve, and set to HIGH for 15 minutes. Open pressure valve to quickly release the pressure.

**Slow Cooker**
Cover and set to HIGH for 2 hours. For best results, stir halfway through.

## 3. GO!

For the thickest glaze, remove the wings and bring glaze up to a simmer (either within your cooker or on the stove for traditional slow cookers) after cooking, letting the glaze reduce to your desired consistency.

**ERIC'S TIP:** Depending on the time of year, this is delicious with fresh pear juice in place of the apple cider.

### INGREDIENTS:

2 pounds chicken wings and drumettes

½ cup fresh apple cider

¼ cup orange marmalade

2 tablespoons butter

2 tablespoons brown sugar

1 tablespoon honey

1 teaspoon black pepper

¼ teaspoon cayenne pepper

salt and pepper to taste

# MOROCCAN WINGS

## SERVES 4—6

## 1. TOSS IT!

Place all ingredients into desired cooker, tossing to combine.

## 2. COOK IT!

**Pressure Cooker**
Lock lid, close pressure valve, and set to HIGH for 15 minutes. Open pressure valve to quickly release the pressure.

**Slow Cooker**
Cover and set to HIGH for 2 hours. For best results, stir halfway through.

## 3. GO!

For the thickest glaze, transfer chicken after cooking and bring the glaze up to a simmer (either within your cooker or on the stove for traditional slow cookers), letting the glaze reduce to your desired consistency. Serve wings covered in the sauce.

**ERIC'S TIP:** These wings go great with a Mediterranean-style lemon dill yogurt instead of the traditional bleu cheese or ranch.

## INGREDIENTS:

2 pounds chicken wings and drumettes

2 tablespoons olive oil

1 tablespoon soy sauce

1 tablespoon honey

3 tablespoons brown sugar

2 teaspoons salt

2 teaspoons black pepper

2 teaspoons ground cinnamon

2 teaspoons ground coriander

2 teaspoons ground cumin

1 teaspoon red pepper flakes

1 teaspoon fresh lemon zest, chopped

¼ teaspoon ground cloves

½ teaspoon ground cardamom

3 cloves garlic, chopped

# MISO AND SOY GLAZED CHICKEN

## SERVES 4-6

## 1. TOSS IT!

Place all ingredients, except cornstarch mixture, into desired cooker, tossing to combine.

## 2. COOK IT!

**Pressure Cooker**
Lock lid, close pressure valve, and set to HIGH for 20 minutes. Open pressure valve to quickly release the pressure.

**Slow Cooker**
Cover and set to LOW for 6 hours.

## 3. GO!

To thicken the glaze, set chicken aside and bring the glaze up to a simmer (either within your cooker or on the stove for traditional slow cookers). Whisk the corn starch mixture into the simmering glaze and let cook 2 minutes, until thickened. Toss chicken in the glaze before serving.

**ERIC'S TIP:** I love to serve this over stir-fried kale or bok choy, cooked with a lot of fresh garlic.

## INGREDIENTS:

2 pounds boneless, skinless chicken thighs

16 ounces whole shiitake mushrooms, stems removed

½ cup chicken stock

3 tablespoons miso paste

3 cloves garlic, chopped

2 tablespoons vermouth or dry sherry (or mirin wine).

2 tablespoons grated fresh ginger

2 tablespoons honey

2 tablespoons soy sauce

1 tablespoon sesame oil

1 tablespoon gochujang or Sriracha sauce

1 tablespoon rice wine vinegar

1 tablespoon cornstarch dissolved in 3 tablespoons cold water

# GREEK CHICKEN AND RICE

## SERVES 4

Mediterranean flavors of lemon, oregano, and Kalamata olives are combined with rice and chicken to create this light yet fulfilling dinner.

## 1. TOSS IT!

Place all ingredients except feta cheese and parsley into desired cooker and toss to combine.

## 2. COOK IT!

**Pressure Cooker**
Lock lid, close pressure valve, and set to HIGH for 6 minutes. Open pressure valve to quickly release the pressure.

**Slow Cooker**
Cover and set to HIGH for 2 hours, or until rice is tender.

## 3. GO!

Let rest for 2 minutes, add the cheese and parsley and fluff with a fork before serving.

**ERIC'S TIP:** For even more color and flavor, add ½ cup diced red bell pepper before cooking.

## INGREDIENTS:

1½ cups long grain white rice, rinsed

1 pound boneless, skinless chicken thighs, chopped into 1-inch cubes

2½ cups water

½ cup sliced Kalamata olives

Zest of 1 lemon

1 teaspoon dried thyme

1 teaspoon garlic powder

1 teaspoon dried oregano

1 tablespoon vegetable oil

½ teaspoon salt

½ teaspoon black pepper

1 cup crumbled feta cheese

1 cup fresh chopped parsley

# CHICKEN TIKKA MASALA

## SERVES 4—6

## 1. TOSS IT!

Place all ingredients, except yogurt, cilantro, and scallions, into desired cooker, tossing to combine.

## 2. COOK IT!

**Pressure Cooker**
Lock lid, close pressure valve, and set to HIGH for 20 minutes. Open pressure valve to quickly release the pressure.

**Slow Cooker**
Cover and set to LOW for 6 hours, or until meat is tender.

## 3. GO!

Stir in yogurt, cilantro, and scallions before serving.

**ERIC'S TIP:** I like to serve this over fragrant jasmine rice cooked with golden raisins.

### INGREDIENTS:

2 pounds boneless, skinless chicken thighs

1 (14.5-ounce) can diced tomatoes, with liquid

1 cup diced onion

1 cup diced green bell pepper

½ cup chicken stock

3 cloves garlic, chopped

3 tablespoons grated ginger

2 tablespoons yellow curry powder

1 tablespoon cumin

1 tablespoon paprika

1 tablespoon Chinese five spice powder

2 teaspoons salt

2 teaspoons black pepper

½ cup plain Greek yogurt

¼ cup chopped fresh cilantro

¼ cup chopped scallions

# COQ AU VIN (EASY CHICKEN STEW)

## SERVES 4–6

This French dish of chicken braised in red wine (typically Burgundy) is perfect for my toss and go treatment, as it is all stewed in the same pot. Let the flavors build themselves and you can give yourself a break… Maybe have a glass of that wine.

## 1. TOSS IT!

Place all ingredients, except butter and dried potato flakes, into desired cooker, tossing to combine.

## 2. COOK IT!

**Pressure Cooker**
Lock lid, close pressure valve, and set to HIGH for 15 minutes. Open pressure valve to quickly release the pressure.

**Slow Cooker**
Cover and set to LOW for 6 hours.

## 3. GO!

Stir in butter and potato flakes before serving. (removing the chicken before adding the butter and potato flakes make it easier to combine).

### INGREDIENTS:

2 pounds boneless, skinless chicken thighs

1 (16-ounce) bag frozen pearl onions

½ cup chopped bacon

1½ cups dry red wine

½ cup dry vermouth or dry sherr

8 ounces button mushrooms, halved

2 cups carrots, sliced

2 tablespoons tomato paste

1 tablespoon light brown sugar

5 sprigs fresh thyme

2 teaspoons minced garlic

1¼ teaspoons salt

1 teaspoon black pepper

1 bay leaf

3 tablespoons butter

¾ cup dried potato flakes

**ERIC'S TIP:** While it would no longer be true Coq au Vin, a similar dish can be prepared without wine by substituting 1½ cups of beef broth and 1 tablespoon of balsamic vinegar in place of the wine.

# CHICKEN SAUSAGE WITH FENNEL

## SERVES 4–6

## 1. TOSS IT!

Place all ingredients, except tarragon, into desired cooker, tossing to combine.

## 2. COOK IT!

**Pressure Cooker**
Lock lid, close pressure valve, and set to HIGH for 15 minutes. Open pressure valve to quickly release the pressure.

**Slow Cooker**
Cover and set to LOW for 6 hours, or until fennel is tender.

## 3. GO!

Add tarragon, tossing all, before serving fennel over bratwurst.

**ERIC'S TIP:** These make great tailgate sandwiches or serve them with mashed Yukon gold potatoes for an updated version of Bangers and Mash.

## INGREDIENTS:

2 pounds raw chicken sausage links

12 ounces beer

2 heads fennel, sliced

1 cup sliced onion

3 cloves garlic, chopped

2 tablespoons Worcestershire sauce

2 tablespoons fennel seed

2 teaspoons caraway seed

1 tablespoon Dijon mustard

1 teaspoon salt

1 teaspoon black pepper

1 bay leaf

3 tablespoons chopped fresh tarragon

# CHICKEN CASSOULET

## SERVES 4—6

## 1. TOSS IT!

Place all ingredients, except chicken, beans, and bacon bits, into desired cooker, whisking to fully incorporate flour.

## 2. COOK IT!

**Pressure Cooker**
Stir in chicken, beans, and bacon bits. Lock lid, close pressure valve, and set to HIGH for 15 minutes. Open pressure valve to quickly release the pressure.

**Slow Cooker**
Stir in chicken, cover, and set to LOW for 6 hours. Stir in beans and bacon bits, cover, and let cook 1 additional hour.

## 3. GO!

Serve alongside crusty bread, if desired.

## INGREDIENTS:

1½ cups chicken stock

1 (14.5-ounce) can petite diced tomatoes, with liquid

1 teaspoon tomato paste

1½ cups pre-diced onions, carrots, and celery.

½ cup white wine

2 tablespoons all-purpose flour

2 teaspoons salt

1 tablespoon minced garlic

1 teaspoon dried thyme

1 teaspoon dried rosemary

1 teaspoon black pepper

3 pounds boneless, skinless chicken thighs

3 (15-ounce) cans cannellini beans, drained and rinsed

½ cup real bacon bits

# CHICKEN CARBONARA PASTA

## SERVES 4–6

While rooted in Italy, where it is made with egg yolk, this American version of Carbonara is a real family favorite using creamy Alfredo sauce in place of those yolks. Chicken, diced ham, and green peas join the pasta to make this a complete meal.

## 1. TOSS IT!

### Pressure Cooker
Add all ingredients, except Parmesan cheese, to the cooker. Add 2½ cups water and stir to combine, ensuring pasta is fully submerged under liquid. NOTE: Once the pasta is completely covered in liquid do not add more water. It's ok if it's less than 2 ½ cups.

### Slow Cooker
Add chicken, Alfredo sauce, peas, ham, chicken stock, olive oil, and garlic to the cooker and stir to combine.

## 2. COOK IT!

### Pressure Cooker
Lock lid, close pressure valve, and set to HIGH for 6 minutes. Open pressure valve to quickly release the pressure.

### Slow Cooker
Cover and set to LOW for 2 hours. Boil the macaroni for ¾ the time recommended on the package. Drain and transfer macaroni to the slow cooker. Cover and cook 1 additional hour.

## 3. GO!

Stir in Parmesan cheese and season with salt and pepper to taste before serving.

## INGREDIENTS:

2 boneless, skinless chicken breasts, cut into ¾-inch cubes

1 (15-ounce) jar prepared Alfredo sauce

1 (10-12-ounce) package frozen peas

8 ounces diced ham

½ cup chicken stock or broth

1 tablespoon olive oil

1 tablespoon minced garlic

12 ounces mezze penne pasta (about 3 cups dry)

1½ cups grated Parmesan cheese

Salt and black pepper

**ERIC'S TIP:** For a little color, top this with a sprinkling of fresh diced tomato and chopped parsley before serving.

# CHICKEN AND RICE VERDE

## SERVES 4

Green salsa verde adds a ton of flavor to this chicken and rice dish made with only a few non-pantry ingredients. Fresh cilantro and lime zest helps brighten up the flavors of the jarred salsa, making it taste fresh without all the prep-work of making salsa from scratch.

## 1. TOSS IT!

Place all ingredients into desired cooker and toss to combine, ensuring rice is below the water level.

## 2. COOK IT!

**Pressure Cooker**
Lock lid, close pressure valve, and set to HIGH for 6 minutes. Open pressure valve to quickly release the pressure.

**Slow Cooker**
Cover and set to HIGH for 2 hours, or until rice is tender and chicken is cooked through.

## 3. GO!

Serve immediately.

**ERIC'S TIP:** For even more flavor, top with shredded pepper-jack cheese before serving.

## INGREDIENTS:

4 boneless, skinless chicken breasts, chopped

1½ cups long grain white rice, rinsed

2½ cups water

½ cup salsa verde

⅓ cup chopped fresh cilantro

Zest and juice of 1 lime

1 tablespoon vegetable oil

¾ teaspoon salt

½ teaspoon black pepper

# CHICKEN AND BACON WITH WILD RICE

## SERVES 4–6

## 1. TOSS IT!

Place all ingredients into desired cooker and toss to combine.

## 2. COOK IT!

**Pressure Cooker**
Lock lid, close pressure valve, and set to HIGH for 30 minutes. Open pressure valve to quickly release the pressure.

**Slow Cooker**
Cover and set to LOW for 8 hours, or until rice is tender and chicken is falling off the bone.

## 3. GO!

Serve immediately.

**INGREDIENTS:**

8 skinless, bone-in chicken thighs

8 ounces wild rice

2 (14.5-ounce) cans diced tomatoes

1 (10.5-ounce) can golden mushroom condensed soup (no water added)

1½ cups chicken stock

½ cup white wine

½ cup chopped cooked bacon

1 cup onion, chopped

1 cup carrot, chopped

1 cup celery, chopped

1 tablespoon dried minced onion

1 teaspoon Worcestershire sauce

1 teaspoon minced garlic

1 teaspoon dried sage

½ teaspoon celery seed

# BOURBON CHICKEN AND BROCCOLI

## SERVES 4—6

One of the most popular takeout dishes around, savory and sweet Bourbon Chicken (sometimes called Bourbon Street Chicken) is paired with broccoli in this recipe for a more satisfying dish you can make in minutes. For a full meal, simply serve over white or brown rice.

## 1. TOSS IT!

Place all ingredients, except hoisin sauce, into desired cooker, tossing to combine.

## 2. COOK IT!

**Pressure Cooker**
Lock lid, close pressure valve, and set to HIGH for 4 minutes. Open pressure valve to quickly release the pressure.

**Slow Cooker**
Cover and set to LOW for 4 hours, or until broccoli is tender.

## 3. GO!

Drain almost all liquid from the cooker, then stir in hoisin sauce before serving.

**ERIC'S TIP:** Hoisin sauce is a lot like Chinese barbecue sauce. It can be purchased in the Asian foods aisle near the soy sauce.

## INGREDIENTS:

1 pound boneless, skinless chicken thighs, chopped into ½-inch cubes

14–16 ounces fresh broccoli florets

½ cup diced red bell pepper

½ cup chicken broth or stock

3 tablespoons soy sauce

2 tablespoons light brown sugar

2 tablespoons bourbon (optional)

2 teaspoons sesame oil

1 teaspoon minced garlic

½ teaspoon onion powder

⅓ cup hoisin sauce

# CHICKEN AND ARTICHOKE PICCATA

## SERVES 4

An Italian favorite with lemon and capers, Chicken Piccata traditionally requires lightly dredging the meat in flour before pan frying and then starting to build the flavors of the sauce. I've given this my "Toss and Go" treatment by eliminating the flour and jumping right into the cooker. To take this classic in a new direction, I've added tender artichoke hearts, which nearly melt into the sauce, adding more flavor and texture.

## 1. TOSS IT!

Place chicken breasts, chicken stock, artichoke hearts, lemon juice, garlic, pepper, and sugar, into desired cooker, tossing to combine.

## 2. COOK IT!

**Pressure Cooker**
Lock lid, close pressure valve, and set to HIGH for 8 minutes. Open pressure valve to quickly release the pressure.

**Slow Cooker**
Cover and set to LOW for 4 hours, or until chicken is cooked through.

## 3. GO!

Stir in butter and capers before serving, topped with grated Parmesan cheese and chopped fresh parsley.

## INGREDIENTS:

4 boneless, skinless chicken breasts

¾ cup chicken stock or broth

1 (14.5-ounce) can quartered artichoke hearts, drained

Juice of 1 lemon

1½ teaspoons minced garlic

1 teaspoon black pepper

¼ teaspoon sugar

6 tablespoons butter

2 tablespoons capers, drained

Grated Parmesan cheese

Chopped fresh parsley

**ERIC'S TIP:** The small amount of added sugar in this recipe can be omitted, though I find that it balances out the acid of the fresh lemon juice.

# BONELESS CHICKEN CACCIATORE

## SERVES 6-8

Using boneless, skinless chicken thighs in this version of a classic Italian dish gives you tender meat that easily pulls apart, without having to worry about the extra steps of browning the chicken skin or removing any bones.

## 1. TOSS IT!

Place all ingredients into desired cooker and toss to combine.

## 2. COOK IT!

**Pressure Cooker**
Lock lid, close pressure valve, and set to HIGH for 15 minutes. Open pressure valve to quickly release the pressure.

**Slow Cooker**
Cover and set to LOW for 6 hours.

## 3. GO!

Serve immediately.

**ERIC'S TIP:** Obviously this recipe is perfect over pasta, as you'd expect from an Italian dish, but it also goes great over white rice.

## INGREDIENTS:

2 pounds boneless, skinless chicken thighs

1 pound ground hot Italian sausage (or cut links into small pieces)

1 (24-ounce) jar prepared pasta sauce

8 ounces baby bella mushrooms, quartered

2 carrots, sliced

1 green bell pepper, chopped

1 cup diced red onion

½ cup chicken stock or broth

1 tablespoon balsamic vinegar

2 teaspoons minced garlic

2 teaspoons dried oregano

¾ teaspoon salt

¾ teaspoon pepper

# BEEF, PORK & LAMB

FRENCH-STYLE SHORT RIBS

BARBECUE COUNTRY RIBS

CARAMELIZED PORK CHOPS WITH CARROTS

PULLED PORK WITH DRIED CHERRIES AND COLA

CARIBBEAN PULLED PORK

CHINESE-STYLE BBQ RIBS

MUSTARD-GLAZED PORK CHOPS

PAN ASIAN RIBS

SWEET SAUSAGE WITH CLAM SAUCE AND RICE

SPIRAL HAM WITH BIRCH BEER

SPANISH-STYLE SAUSAGE

SOUTH PHILLY HOT SAUSAGE

SODA POP BRAISED PORK

HAWAIIAN SWEET AND SOUR SHORT RIBS

BARBECUE BEEF SANDWICHES

KOREAN BRAISED SHORT RIBS

SHEPHERD'S STEW

BEEF BRISKET WITH FENNEL

MOM-WICH SLOPPY JOES

POT ROAST WITH MASHED POTATOES AND GRAVY

SWEET AND SOUR MEATBALLS

SIRLOIN STEAK TIPS

BRAISED LAMB SHANKS

# FRENCH-STYLE SHORT RIBS

## SERVES 4–6

## 1. TOSS IT!

Place all ingredients, except thyme and potato flakes, into desired cooker, tossing to combine.

## 2. COOK IT!

**Pressure Cooker**
Lock lid, close pressure valve, and set to HIGH for 45 minutes. Open pressure valve to quickly release the pressure.

**Slow Cooker**
Cover and set to LOW for 8–10 hours, until beef is tender.

## 3. GO!

Add the potato flakes to thicken. Serve garnished with thyme.

## INGREDIENTS:

4 pounds beef short ribs

2 cups shallots, peeled and sliced in half lengthwise

2 cups prunes, roughly chopped

2 tablespoons butter

1 cup red wine

½ cup beef stock

1 teaspoon salt

1 teaspoon black pepper

1 cinnamon stick

1 teaspoon chopped fresh thyme

½ cup dried potato flakes

# BARBECUE COUNTRY RIBS

## SERVES 4–6

The vinegar and mustard complement the sweetness of the sauce in this recipe, which is characteristic to Carolina Barbecue.

## 1. TOSS IT!

Place all ingredients into desired cooker, tossing to combine.

## 2. COOK IT!

**Pressure Cooker**
Lock lid, close pressure valve, and set to HIGH for 20 minutes. Open pressure valve to quickly release the pressure.

**Slow Cooker**
Cover and set to LOW for 6–8 hours, until meat is tender and falling off the bone.

## 3. GO!

Serve immediately.

**ERIC'S TIP:** You can also use pork loin chops in place of the ribs in this recipe, as these cuts of pork require less cooking time to become tender.

## INGREDIENTS:

4 pounds country-style pork ribs, bone in

1 onion, sliced

¼ cup BBQ sauce

¼ cup red wine vinegar

2 tablespoons mustard

½ cup peach jelly

¼ cup dark brown sugar

3 tablespoons garlic, chopped

3 teaspoons salt

2 teaspoons black pepper

# CARAMELIZED PORK CHOPS WITH CARROTS

## SERVES 4

These pork chops use molasses and soy sauce to create a flavorful glaze to help brown the chops using only the heat of the cooker, without any additional browning step! Glazed carrots are cooked atop the chops to help complete the meal.

## 1. TOSS IT!

Place pork chops, molasses, soy sauce, brown sugar, water, and pepper into desired cooker, tossing to fully coat the chops. Top the chops with the carrots and butter.

## 2. COOK IT!

**Pressure Cooker**
Lock lid, close pressure valve, and set to HIGH for 2 minutes. Let the pressure release naturally 5 minutes before releasing the remaining pressure.

**Slow Cooker**
Cover and set to LOW for 6 hours, until carrots and chops are tender.

## 3. GO!

Toss the pork chops and carrots in the sauce to coat before serving.

### INGREDIENTS:

4 center-cut pork loin chops (1-inch thick)

¼ cup molasses

2 tablespoons soy sauce

2 tablespoons light brown sugar

2 tablespoons water

½ teaspoon black pepper

1 pound baby carrots

2 tablespoons butter

**ERIC'S TIP:** For a nice maple flavor, maple syrup can be used in place of the molasses, however the glaze won't be as thick.

# PULLED PORK WITH DRIED CHERRIES AND COLA

## SERVES 6—8

## 1. TOSS IT!

Place all ingredients into desired cooker, tossing to combine.

## 2. COOK IT!

**Pressure Cooker**
Lock lid, close pressure valve, and set to HIGH for 60 minutes. Open pressure valve to quickly release the pressure.

**Slow Cooker**
Cover and set to LOW for 8 hours, or until pork shreds easily.

## 3. GO!

Use two forks to shred the pork into the cooking liquid before seasoning with salt to taste.

## INGREDIENTS:

1 boneless pork shoulder, cut into 4 pieces

1 (12-ounce) can cola

1 onion, sliced

1 (6-ounce) bag dried cherries

1 cup cherry jelly

½ cup dark brown sugar

½ cup soy sauce

3 tablespoons chopped garlic

1 tablespoon fennel seed

2 teaspoons black pepper

Salt, to taste

**ERIC'S TIP:** The cut of meat labeled "pork butt" actually comes from the top of the shoulder, while the "shoulder roast" is cut from the bottom of the shoulder. I prefer the shoulder roast because it has a richer flavor, as well as a higher fat content that lends to a more mouthwatering result.

# CARIBBEAN PULLED PORK

## SERVES 6-8

This totally unique take on pulled pork is guaranteed to transport you to the tropics, as these flavors are based on the popular Cuban marinade, mojo criollo, with an added touch of Jamaican allspice.

## 1. TOSS IT!

Place all ingredients into desired cooker, tossing to combine.

## 2. COOK IT!

**Pressure Cooker**
Lock lid, close pressure valve, and set to HIGH for 60 minutes. Let the pressure release naturally for 15 minutes before opening valve to release remaining pressure.

**Slow Cooker**
Cover and set to LOW for 8 hours, or until pork shreds easily.

## 3. GO!

Use two forks to shred the pork into the cooking liquid before serving.

**ERIC'S TIP:** This pulled pork is great on its own, served with a side of black beans, yellow rice, and a few lime wedges to squeeze over the top, or on Hawaiian buns with slices of fresh avocado.

## INGREDIENTS:

1 (3-4 pound) boneless pork shoulder or butt roast, cut into 4 equal pieces

½ cup chicken stock

½ cup orange juice

1 tablespoon sugar

1 tablespoon minced garlic

2 teaspoons dried oregano

2 teaspoons salt

1½ teaspoons black pepper

1 teaspoon orange zest

¾ teaspoon ground allspice

½ cup potato flakes

# CHINESE-STYLE BBQ RIBS

## SERVES 4–6

## 1. TOSS IT!

Place all ingredients, except scallions and sesame seeds, into desired cooker, tossing to combine.

## 2. COOK IT!

**Pressure Cooker**
Lock lid, close pressure valve, and set to HIGH for 20 minutes. Open pressure valve to quickly release the pressure.

**Slow Cooker**
Cover and set to LOW for 6 hours, or until ribs are tender.

## 3. GO!

For the thickest glaze, after cooking, remove ribs and bring the glaze up to a simmer (either within your cooker or on the stove for traditional slow cookers), letting the glaze reduce until your desired consistency. Toss ribs in glaze before serving, garnished with scallions and sesame seeds.

**ERIC'S TIP:** This type of Cantonese BBQ is called Char Siu. It's sweet, aromatic, and glazed with a hint of ginger. To get that traditional red tint you'd get in a restaurant, add 1 teaspoon red food coloring before cooking.

### INGREDIENTS:

2 racks baby back ribs, cut into two-rib pieces

½ cup brown sugar

½ cup bourbon or brandy

¼ cup honey

3 tablespoons hoisin sauce

3 tablespoons soy sauce

3 tablespoons sesame oil

3 tablespoons chopped garlic

2 tablespoons chopped ginger

1 tablespoon Chinese five spice powder

2 teaspoons salt

2 teaspoons black pepper

¼ cup chopped scallions

2 tablespoons toasted sesame seeds

# MUSTARD GLAZED PORK CHOPS

## SERVES 4

Tender center-cut pork chops are topped with a sweet and savory mustard glaze in this simple entrée you can prep in mere minutes.

## 1. TOSS IT!

Place chicken stock, sage, and onion powder into desired cooker, stirring to combine. Whisk together mustard and sugar and spread evenly over the top of each pork chop.

## 2. COOK IT!

**Pressure Cooker**
Position a steamer insert above liquid in cooker. Place the pork chops atop the insert, glaze-side up. Lock lid, close pressure valve, and set to HIGH for 15 minutes. Let the pressure release naturally for 5 minutes before opening valve to release remaining pressure.

**Slow Cooker**
Place the pork chops, glaze-side up, directly into the liquid in the cooker. Cover and set to LOW for 6 hours.

## 3. GO!

Serve immediately.

### INGREDIENTS:

1 cup chicken stock or broth

4 leaves sage

1/2 teaspoon onion powder

4 (thick-cut) pork loin chops, about 1-inch thick

1/3 cup coarse deli mustard

2 tablespoons sugar

**ERIC'S TIP:** While some coarse ground mustards can be very spicy, fancy mustard with visible seeds, is usually far more mild.

# PAN ASIAN RIBS

## SERVES 4–6

## 1. TOSS IT!

Place all ingredients, except cornstarch mixture, into desired cooker, tossing to combine.

## 2. COOK IT!

**Pressure Cooker**
Lock lid, close pressure valve, and set to HIGH for 30 minutes. Open pressure valve to quickly release the pressure.

**Slow Cooker**
Cover and set to LOW for 6 hours, or until tender.

## 3. GO!

To thicken the glaze, set ribs aside and bring the glaze up to a simmer (either within your cooker or on the stove for traditional slow cookers). Whisk the cornstarch mixture into the simmering glaze and let cook 2 minutes, until thickened. Toss ribs in the glaze before serving.

**ERIC'S TIP:** Any type of pork rib cut will work with this recipe, but my preference is the St. Louis style. These ribs have more meat and a higher fat content than baby back ribs which equals more flavor! If you use standard spare ribs, increase the cooking time to 35 minutes in the pressure cooker and 7 hours in the slow cooker.

## INGREDIENTS:

2 racks of St Louis pork ribs (spare ribs), cut into 2 rib pieces

½ cup orange juice

¼ cup orange juice concentrate

¼ cup soy sauce

¼ cup honey

3 tablespoons sesame oil

2 tablespoons chopped fresh ginger

2 tablespoons red curry paste

2 tablespoons brown sugar

2 tablespoons lemongrass paste

2 teaspoons black pepper

1 tablespoon cornstarch whisked into 3 tablespoons cold water

# SWEET SAUSAGE WITH CLAM SAUCE AND RICE

## SERVES 4

## 1. TOSS IT!

Place all ingredients, except tomato and parsley, into desired cooker, tossing to combine.

## 2. COOK IT!

**Pressure Cooker**
Lock lid, close pressure valve, and set to HIGH for 8 minutes. Open pressure valve to quickly release the pressure.

**Slow Cooker**
Cover and set to HIGH for 2 hours. For best results, stir halfway through.

## 3. GO!

Season with salt and pepper to taste before serving topped with fresh tomato and parsley.

## INGREDIENTS:

1 pound ground sweet Italian sausage, broken up

2 cups chicken stock

1 (15-ounce) can white clam sauce

12 ounces frozen broccoli florets

1½ cups basmati rice

1 cup frozen corn kernels

1 cup white wine

¼ cup sweet vermouth

1 tablespoon butter

1 teaspoon dried thyme

1 teaspoon dried oregano

Salt and black pepper to taste

1 cup diced fresh tomato

½ cup chopped fresh parsley

# SPIRAL HAM WITH BIRCH BEER

## SERVES 4–6

## 1. TOSS IT!

Place ham into desired cooker. Whisk together birch beer, sugar, mustard, five spice powder, salt, and pepper, and pour over the top.

## 2. COOK IT!

**Pressure Cooker**
Lock lid, close pressure valve, and set to HIGH for 25 minutes. Open pressure valve to quickly release the pressure.

**Slow Cooker**
Cover and set to LOW for 4 hours.

## 3. GO!

Set aside ham and stir cookie crumbs into the glaze, until cookies have completely dissolved and glaze has thickened. To serve, drizzle glaze over slices of the ham.

### INGREDIENTS:

1 (5-pound) spiral-cut ham

24 ounces birch beer

½ cup dark brown sugar

3 tablespoons English mustard

2 teaspoons Chinese five spice powder

2 teaspoons salt

2 teaspoons black pepper

1 cup crushed gingersnap cookies

**ERIC'S TIP:** If you can't find a spiral-cut ham, you can substitute a regular bone-in cured ham. Just increase the cooking time to 45 minutes for the pressure cooker and 5 hours in the slow cooker. The gingersnap cookies will help thicken sauce on top of adding an extra dimension of flavor. I like to chop leftover ham in my food processor and add mayonnaise, relish, and mustard to make ham salad for sandwiches the next day.

# SPANISH-STYLE SAUSAGE

## SERVES 8

## 1. TOSS IT!

Oil desired cooker with the olive oil before adding all remaining ingredients, except for Serving and Garnish. Toss to combine.

## 2. COOK IT!

**Pressure Cooker**
Lock lid, close pressure valve, and set to HIGH for 15 minutes. Open pressure valve to quickly release the pressure.

**Slow Cooker**
Cover and set to LOW for 4 hours, or until sausage is cooked through.

## 3. GO!

Season the sausage mixture with salt and pepper to taste. To serve, top naan bread with sausage and other ingredients from the cooker, then top that with Manchego cheese and arugula. Drizzle balsamic glaze and sprinkle lightly with salt and pepper.

**ERIC'S TIP:** This is also great when served over crusty Italian bread in place of the naan. You will likely have a large amount of sauce leftover once the sausage is gone but I like to save that and use it as a homemade pasta sauce for an entire second meal!

## INGREDIENTS:

2 tablespoons olive oil

3 pounds hot sausage links, such as chorizo or Italian

4 onions, sliced

1 (28-ounce) can San Marzano peeled tomatoes

1 (15-ounce) can garbanzo beans, drained and rinsed

1 cup sliced roasted red peppers

1 cup sweet vermouth

Juice of 1 lemon

¼ cup paprika

2 tablespoons tomato paste

1 tablespoon balsamic vinegar

1 tablespoon chopped garlic

1 teaspoon dried oregano

1 teaspoon dried thyme

Salt and black pepper to taste

**SERVING AND GARNISH**

Naan bread (about 8 rounds, halved)

1 pound Manchego cheese, grated

Baby arugula

Balsamic glaze

# SOUTH PHILLY HOT SAUSAGE

## SERVES 4–6

## 1. TOSS IT!

Place all ingredients except cheese into desired cooker, tossing to combine.

## 2. COOK IT!

### Pressure Cooker
Lock lid, close pressure valve, and set to HIGH for 15 minutes. Open pressure valve to quickly release the pressure.

### Slow Cooker
Cover and set to LOW for 4–6 hours, until broccoli rabe is very tender.

## 3. GO!

Place a thick slice of provolone cheese on the bun then add the sausage mixture.

### INGREDIENTS:

2 pounds hot Italian sausage links

1-2 bunches broccoli rabe, stems trimmed

2 long hot peppers, sliced

1 onion, sliced

1 cup beef stock

3 tablespoons chopped garlic

2 teaspoons salt

2 teaspoons black pepper

4-6 thick slices of provolone

**ERIC'S TIP:** This is a very intense and spicy dish. You can tame the heat by using sweet Italian sausage and removing the long hot peppers.

# SODA POP BRAISED PORK

## SERVES 6–8

## 1. TOSS IT!

Place all ingredients, except pork, salt, and pepper, into desired cooker, mixing until well combined. Add pork to the mixture.

## 2. COOK IT!

**Pressure Cooker**
Lock lid, close pressure valve, and set to HIGH for 60 minutes. Let the pressure release naturally before removing lid.

**Slow Cooker**
Cover and set to LOW for 8 hours, or until pork shreds easily.

## 3. GO!

Use two forks to shred the pork into the cooking liquid before seasoning with salt and pepper to taste.

**ERIC'S TIP:** For added brightness and texture, try topping this dish with finely diced apple.

## INGREDIENTS:

3 cups Dr. Pepper

1 cup chopped white onion

3 cloves garlic, crushed

½ cup ketchup

½ cup chopped dried figs (may use raisins)

⅓ cup apple butter

¼ cup cider vinegar

3 tablespoons olive oil

2 tablespoons soy sauce

2 teaspoons fennel seed

1 teaspoon dried oregano

3½ pounds boneless pork shoulder, cut into 2 or 3 pieces

Salt and black pepper, to taste

# HAWAIIAN SWEET AND SOUR SHORT RIBS

## SERVES 4–6

## 1. TOSS IT!

Generously rub ribs with salt, pepper, and five-spice powder. Place all remaining ingredients, except scallions and sesame seeds, into desired cooker, stirring to combine. Add rubbed ribs to the marinade and toss to coat.

## 2. COOK IT!

**Pressure Cooker**
Lock lid, close pressure valve, and set to HIGH for 40 minutes. Let the pressure release naturally before removing lid.

**Slow Cooker**
Cover and set to LOW for 8–10 hours, until beef is tender.

## 3. GO!

Serve garnished with scallions and toasted sesame seeds.

### INGREDIENTS:

3½ pounds beef short ribs

Salt and black pepper

2 tablespoons Chinese five-spice powder

2 cups onion, large diced

1 cup green bell pepper, large diced

1 (14-ounce) can crushed pineapple with juice

1 cup orange juice

⅓ cup malt vinegar

⅓ cup ketchup

¼ cup honey

3 tablespoons sesame oil

1 clove garlic

3 tablespoons minced fresh ginger

¼ cup chopped scallions

1 tablespoon toasted sesame seeds

# BARBECUE BEEF SANDWICHES

## SERVES 6

With only a handful of ingredients (which even includes the buns) you can make these sandwiches brimming with tender, sweet, and savory pulled beef.

## 1. TOSS IT!

Place chuck roast, ½ of the barbecue sauce, onion, water, brown sugar, salt, and pepper, into desired cooker, tossing to coat the meat.

## 2. COOK IT!

**Pressure Cooker**
Lock lid, close pressure valve, and set to HIGH for 60 minutes. Let the pressure release naturally for 10 minutes before opening valve to release remaining pressure.

**Slow Cooker**
Cover and set to LOW for 8–10 hours, until meat shreds easily.

## 3. GO!

Drain most of the liquid from the cooker and add the remaining ½ of the barbecue sauce. Use two forks to shred the meat into the sauce before serving on hamburger buns.

> **ERIC'S TIP:** When dicing the red onion, thinly slice the other half of the onion to top the sandwiches.

### INGREDIENTS:

1 (3-pound) chuck roast, cut into 4 pieces

1 (18-ounce) bottle barbecue sauce, divided

1 red onion, diced

½ cup orange juice

¼ cup light brown sugar

1¼ teaspoon salt

1 teaspoon black pepper

Hamburger buns

# KOREAN BRAISED SHORT RIBS

## SERVES 6

## 1. TOSS IT!

Place all ingredients, except scallions and cilantro, into desired cooker, tossing to combine.

## 2. COOK IT!

**Pressure Cooker**
Lock lid, close pressure valve, and set to HIGH for 45 minutes. Open pressure valve to quickly release the pressure.

**Slow Cooker**
Cover and set to LOW for 8–10 hours, until beef is tender.

## 3. GO!

Serve garnished with scallions and cilantro.

### INGREDIENTS:

4 pounds beef short ribs

½ head green cabbage, cut into 6 wedges

1 onion, sliced

1 cup beef stock

¼ cup rice wine vinegar

¼ cup soy sauce

3 tablespoons chopped garlic

3 tablespoons tomato paste

3 tablespoons chopped ginger

3 tablespoons gochujang sauce

2 tablespoons sesame oil

2 tablespoons paprika

2 teaspoons salt

2 teaspoons black pepper

¼ cup chopped scallions

¼ cup chopped fresh cilantro

**ERIC'S TIP:** Gochujang is a Korean fermented red chili sauce that is slightly less spicy than Sriracha sauce. I find the flavor a little more complex as well. In my house, gochujang has replaced ketchup as my favorite all-purpose condiment!

# SHEPHERD'S STEW

## SERVES 6

## 1. TOSS IT!

Place all ingredients into desired cooker and toss to combine.

## 2. COOK IT!

### Pressure Cooker
Lock lid, close pressure valve, and set to HIGH for 10 minutes. Open pressure valve to quickly release the pressure.

### Slow Cooker
Cover and set to LOW for 6 hours.

## 3. GO!

Stir well and season with salt and pepper to taste before serving.

## INGREDIENTS:

3 pounds lean ground beef, broken up

2 pounds prepared mashed potatoes

1 (10.5-ounce) can beef consommé

2 cups onion, chopped

1 cup carrots, chopped

1 cup celery, chopped

1 cup frozen peas

1 cup frozen corn kernels

½ cup half and half

1 packet dry Italian salad dressing mix

2 tablespoons ketchup

1 tablespoon tomato paste

1 clove garlic, crushed

1 teaspoon Worcestershire sauce

½ teaspoon paprika

Salt and pepper to taste

# BEEF BRISKET WITH FENNEL

## SERVES 6—8

## 1. TOSS IT!

Place all ingredients, except butter, heavy cream, potato flakes, and parsley, into desired cooker, tossing to combine.

## 2. COOK IT!

**Pressure Cooker**
Lock lid, close pressure valve, and set to HIGH for 60 minutes. Open pressure valve to quickly release the pressure.

**Slow Cooker**
Cover and set to LOW for 8–10 hours, until beef is tender.

## 3. GO!

Transfer the meat to a covered dish and set aside. Add butter, heavy cream, and potato flakes to the cooker, stirring until the sauce has thickened. Serve brisket sliced with a ladling of sauce, garnished with fresh parsley.

**ERIC'S TIP:** If you have the time, searing the meat in preheated olive oil until browned before tossing in the rest of the ingredients in the first step will add another level of flavor to this recipe.

## INGREDIENTS:

3 tablespoons olive oil

4 pounds beef brisket, cut into 4 to 6 pieces

3 cups thinly sliced fennel

2 cups sliced carrots

1 cup roasted red peppers, sliced

¾ cup dry white wine

1 pound baby Yukon gold potatoes

1 teaspoon thyme

2 teaspoons fennel seed

2 teaspoons Worcestershire sauce

1½ cups beef stock

3 tablespoons tomato paste

1 tablespoon minced garlic

1 tablespoon black pepper

1 tablespoon butter

¼ cup heavy cream

¼ cup potato flakes

Fresh Italian parsley, chopped, for garnish

# MOM-WICH SLOPPY JOES

## SERVES 4–6

## 1. TOSS IT!

Place all ingredients into desired cooker, breaking up the ground beef as you toss together.

## 2. COOK IT!

**Pressure Cooker**
Lock lid, close pressure valve, and set to HIGH for 15 minutes. Open pressure valve to quickly release the pressure.

**Slow Cooker**
Cover and set to LOW for 6 hours.

## 3. GO!

Serve on buttered hamburger buns with pickles and/or sliced red onion, if desired.

### INGREDIENTS:

2 pounds very lean ground beef

2 cups chili sauce or ketchup

1 teaspoon yellow mustard

1 teaspoon hot chili sauce

1 cup diced onion

1 (4-ounce) can chopped green chilis

2 tablespoons Worcestershire sauce

2 tablespoons chopped garlic

1 tablespoon salt

2 teaspoons black pepper

**ERIC'S TIP:** I love taking the leftovers and making a Sloppy Joe Shepherd's Pie by filling a casserole dish, topping with biscuits, and baking at the recommended temperature of the biscuits, just until they are golden brown.

# POT ROAST WITH MASHED POTATOES AND GRAVY

## SERVES 4—6

## 1. TOSS IT!

Place soup, stock, onion, celery, wine, rosemary, thyme, dried onion, and garlic into desired cooker and stir to combine. Add chuck roast and ladle gravy over the roast to coat.

## 2. COOK IT!

**Pressure Cooker**
Lock lid, close pressure valve, and set to HIGH for 40 minutes. Allow the pressure to fully release naturally before opening.

**Slow Cooker**
Cover and set to LOW for 6 hours, or until roast is tender, but not falling apart.

## 3. GO!

Transfer roast to a serving platter and let rest 5 minutes before slicing. Meanwhile, stir butter into the gravy. Transfer 2½ cups of the gravy to a serving dish. Stir the potato flakes into the remaining gravy in the cooker to create the mashed potatoes. Serve the sliced meat with the mashed potatoes, covered in the reserved gravy.

## INGREDIENTS:

2 (10.5-ounce) cans condensed cream of broccoli soup (no water added)

2 cups beef stock

1 cup chopped onion

1 cup chopped celery

1 cup red wine

1 teaspoon dried rosemary

1 teaspoon dried thyme

1 tablespoon minced dried onion

2 cloves garlic, crushed

1 beef chuck roast (about 3.5 pounds)

2 tablespoons butter

3 cups instant mashed potato flakes

# SWEET AND SOUR MEATBALLS

## SERVES 4–6

A party-staple, Sweet and Sour Meatballs have never been made easier! Plus, after cooking, you can leave them in a slow cooker or switch a pressure cooker to a "slow cook" or "warm" setting to keep these out at your party for hours… That is, if they aren't all gone in the first few minutes.

## 1. TOSS IT!

Place all meatballs, ketchup, pineapple juice (reserve chunks), bell pepper, onion, soy sauce, onion powder, and pepper, into desired cooker, tossing to combine.

## 2. COOK IT!

**Pressure Cooker**
Lock lid, close pressure valve, and set to HIGH for 6 minutes. Open pressure valve to quickly release the pressure. Stir in brown sugar.

**Slow Cooker**
Fold in pineapple chunks before serving.

## 3. GO!

Serve immediately.

**ERIC'S TIP:** For the best flavor, when purchasing frozen meatballs, look for traditional meatballs, not "Italian" seasoned.

### INGREDIENTS:

32 ounces frozen meatballs

1 cup ketchup

1 (20-ounce) can pineapple chunks in 100% juice, juice separated

⅔ cup diced red bell pepper

½ cup diced yellow onion

3 tablespoons soy sauce

¾ teaspoon onion powder

¾ teaspoon black pepper

¼ cup light brown sugar

# SIRLOIN STEAK TIPS

## SERVES 6

These tender steak tips in a creamy gravy are a simple entrée made from a sirloin tip roast and pantry staples that you likely already have on hand. For a full meal, serve over rice and with a salad or green vegetable.

## 1. TOSS IT!

Place all ingredients, except heavy cream, tomato paste, and Dijon mustard, into desired cooker, tossing to combine.

## 2. COOK IT!

**Pressure Cooker**
Lock lid, close pressure valve, and set to HIGH for 15 minutes. Let the pressure release naturally for 10 minutes before opening valve to release remaining pressure.

**Slow Cooker**
Cover and set to LOW for 6 hours, or until beef is tender.

## 3. GO!

Drain ¾ of the liquid from the cooker, then stir in heavy cream, tomato paste, and Dijon mustard before serving.

> **ERIC'S TIP:** For a thicker gravy, bring the steak and gravy up to a simmer (either within your cooker or on the stove for traditional slow cookers) after cooking, letting the gravy reduce to your desired consistency.

## INGREDIENTS:

1 sirloin tip roast (3½ to 4 pounds), cut into 1-inch cubes

1 cup beef stock

1 cup canned French onion soup

1 cup diced red onion

2 teaspoons minced garlic

1 teaspoon sugar

1 teaspoon salt

1 teaspoon black pepper

½ teaspoon ground mustard

½ cup heavy cream

1 tablespoon tomato paste

2 teaspoons Dijon mustard

# BRAISED LAMB SHANKS

## SERVES 4–6

## 1. TOSS IT!

Place all ingredients, except potato flakes, into desired cooker and toss to combine.

## 2. COOK IT!

**Pressure Cooker**
Lock lid, close pressure valve, and set to HIGH for 35 minutes. Open pressure valve to quickly release the pressure.

**Slow Cooker**
Cover and set to LOW for 8 hours, or until lamb is very tender.

## 3. GO!

Stir in potato flakes to thicken. Stir in chopped mint. For a full meal, serve over a risotto, mashed or roasted potatoes, or even pasta.

**ERIC'S TIP:** If lamb shanks are unavailable, you can use another cut of lamb, like shoulder chops, or even substitute beef short ribs.

### INGREDIENTS:

4 lamb shanks

1 (14.5-ounce) can diced tomatoes

1 cup beef stock

8 oz dried shiitake mushrooms,

1 ounce dried porcini mushrooms

¼ cup sundried tomatoes, chopped

2 tablespoons Worcestershire sauce

1 tablespoon chopped garlic

1 teaspoon salt

1 teaspoon black pepper

¼ teaspoon crushed red pepper flakes

½ cup chopped mint

½ cup dried potato flakes for finishing

# SEAFOOD

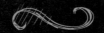

SWEET CHILI MUSSELS

SPICY MUSSELS

LOUISIANA SHRIMP AND SAUSAGE

SHRIMP SCAMPI WITH RICE

LEMON AND DILL FISH FILLETS WITH BABY POTATOES

CHORIZO RICE SCALLOPS

BRUSCHETTA SEA BASS WITH GARLIC GREEN BEANS

CEDAR PLANK GROUPER

# SWEET CHILI MUSSELS

## SERVES 6

## 1. TOSS IT!

Place all ingredients, except heavy cream, cilantro, and lime zest, into desired cooker, tossing to combine.

## 2. COOK IT!

**Pressure Cooker**
Lock lid, close pressure valve, and set to HIGH for 3 minutes. Open pressure valve to quickly release the pressure.

**Slow Cooker**
Cover and set to HIGH for 30 minutes, just until mussels have opened.

## 3. GO!

Using a slotted spoon, transfer mussels to a serving dish. Discard any mussels that have not opened. Stir heavy cream, cilantro, and lime zest into the liquid in the cooker. Season with salt and pepper to taste before pouring over the mussels to serve.

## INGREDIENTS:

4 pounds mussels, scrubbed and de-bearded

2 cups white wine

1 cup chicken stock

1 cup sweet chili sauce

¼ cup hoisin sauce

4 scallions, ½-inch sliced

3 tablespoons olive oil

1 clove garlic, crushed

2 tablespoons chopped fresh ginger

2 tablespoons Chinese mustard

1 cup heavy cream

3 tablespoons chopped fresh cilantro

1 teaspoon lime zest

Salt and black pepper, to taste

# SPICY MUSSELS

## SERVES 6

## 1. TOSS IT!

Place all ingredients, except alfredo sauce, salt, and pepper, into desired cooker, tossing to combine.

## 2. COOK IT!

**Pressure Cooker**
Lock lid, close pressure valve, and set to HIGH for 3 minutes. Open pressure valve to quickly release the pressure.

**Slow Cooker**
Cover and set to HIGH for 30 minutes, just until mussels have opened.

## 3. GO!

Using a slotted spoon, transfer mussels to a serving dish. Discard any mussels that have not opened. Stir alfredo sauce into the liquid in the cooker. Season with salt and pepper to taste before pouring over the mussels to serve.

**ERIC'S TIP:** Proper care for the mussels is crucial for their shelf life. After cleaning, keep on ice in a strainer to let the excess liquid drain. They also need good airflow to stay alive. Discard any mussels that have broken shells or are not closed before cooking.

## INGREDIENTS:

2 pounds mussels, scrubbed and de-bearded

8 ounces pancetta or spec

1 cup white wine or dry vermouth

¼ cup dried porcini mushrooms, chopped

¼ cup sundried tomatoes, chopped

3 tablespoons chopped fresh garlic

1 jalapeño pepper, chopped

½ cup prepared alfredo sauce

Salt and black pepper, to taste

# LOUISIANA SHRIMP AND SAUSAGE

## SERVES 6

This Cajun dish of shrimp, smoked sausage, tomatoes, and okra, is a lot like a gumbo, without the need for a complicated roux to thicken it. For a true Louisiana meal, serve over white rice.

## 1. TOSS IT!

Place all ingredients, except shrimp, into desired cooker, tossing to combine.

## 2. COOK IT!

**Pressure Cooker**
Top ingredients in the cooker with the shrimp. Lock lid, close pressure valve, and set to HIGH for 2 minutes. Open pressure valve to quickly release the pressure.

**Slow Cooker**
Cover and set to LOW for 4 hours. Stir in shrimp, cover, and cook an additional hour, just until shrimp are heated through.

## 3. GO!

Serve immediately.

**ERIC'S TIP:** This is best with a cured andouille or smoked sausage that is fully cooked when you purchase it, not raw, as the fully-cooked sausage will hold its shape better in the final dish.

## INGREDIENTS:

8 ounces andouille or smoked sausage, sliced

1 (14.5-ounce) can diced tomatoes, drained

2 cups frozen cut okra

1 cup green bell pepper, chopped

1 cup celery, diced

1 cup sliced green onions

½ cup chicken stock

1 tablespoon butter

2 teaspoons minced garlic

2 teaspoons creole or Cajun seasoning

1 bay leaf

½ teaspoon dried thyme

1 pound large frozen shrimp

# SHRIMP SCAMPI WITH RICE

## SERVES 4–6

## 1. TOSS IT!

Place all ingredients, except the parsley, and lemon into desired cooker and toss to combine.

## 2. COOK IT!

**Pressure Cooker**
Lock lid, close pressure valve, and set to HIGH for 6 minutes. Open pressure valve to quickly release the pressure.

**Slow Cooker**
Cover and set to HIGH for 1 hour. Stir in shrimp, cover, and cook an additional 30 minutes.

## 3. GO!

Stir in parsley, lemon zest, and lemon juice before serving.

## INGREDIENTS:

3 cups shrimp or chicken stock

2 cups Arborio rice

1 cup clam juice

½ cup white wine

2 tablespoons chopped garlic

3 tablespoons butter

1 teaspoon salt

1 teaspoon black pepper

1 ½ pounds frozen peeled and deveined shrimp

½ cup fresh parsley, chopped

1 teaspoon red pepper flakes

Zest and juice of 2 lemons

**ERIC'S TIP:** I always like to keep a big bag of IQF (Individually Quick Frozen) shrimp in the freezer. You can take out only what you need and keep the rest for your next creation!

# LEMON AND DILL FISH FILLETS WITH BABY POTATOES

## SERVES 2

These white fish fillets are topped with whole sprigs of dill and whole slices of lemon, creating a beautiful presentation (just remember to move the lemon aside before eating). This tried and true combination of flavors is so simple, that this recipe even includes buttered baby potatoes cooked alongside the fish, and still boasts only 5 non-pantry ingredients.

## 1. TOSS IT!

**Pressure Cooker**

Place potatoes, water, chopped dill, and 1 tablespoon of the butter into the cooker. Lightly season with salt and pepper. Place a steamer insert on top and top with the fish fillets. Season each fillet with salt and pepper before topping with a tablespoon of butter, sprig of dill, and 3 slices of the lemon.

**Slow Cooker**

Place potatoes, water, chopped dill, and 1 tablespoon of the butter in the cooker. Lightly season with salt and pepper.

## 2. COOK IT!

**Pressure Cooker**

Lock lid, close pressure valve, and set to HIGH for 4 minutes. Open pressure valve to quickly release the pressure.

**Slow Cooker**

Cover and set to LOW for 3 hours. Top potatoes with fish fillets. Season each fillet with salt and pepper before topping with a tablespoon of butter, sprig of dill, and 3 slices of the lemon. Cover and cook an additional 2 hours, or until fish is tender and flaky.

## 3. GO!

Serve the fish fillets alongside or over the dill potatoes. Sprinkle with fresh chopped parsley.

## INGREDIENTS:

1 pound baby potatoes, quartered

½ cup water

1 tablespoon chopped fresh dill, plus 2 sprigs

3 tablespoons butter, divided

Salt and black pepper

2 8 oz frozen white fish fillets (cod recommended)

6 thin slices lemon

½ cup fresh parsley, chopped (garnish)

**ERIC'S TIP:** For the best presentation, I use multi-colored baby potatoes. I also serve this with additional lemon wedges to squeeze over the fish.

# CHORIZO RICE SCALLOPS

## SERVES 4–6

## 1. TOSS IT!

Place all ingredients, except scallops, into desired cooker, tossing to combine.

## 2. COOK IT!

### Pressure Cooker
Top ingredients in the cooker with the scallops. Lock lid, close pressure valve, and set to HIGH for 6 minutes. Open pressure valve to quickly release the pressure.

### Slow Cooker
Cover and set to HIGH for 2 hours, adding scallops in the last 30 minutes.

## 3. GO!

Serve immediately.

## INGREDIENTS:

1 pound raw chorizo, broken up

4 cups chicken stock

2 cups Jasmine rice

1 green bell pepper, chopped

1 cup chopped onion

½ cup chopped celery

½ cup chopped carrots

2 tablespoons chopped garlic

2 tablespoons butter

1 tablespoon paprika

2 teaspoons cumin

1 teaspoon salt

1 teaspoon black pepper

1 pound sea scallops

**ERIC'S TIP:** If you want to kick up the spice, add 2 tablespoons of chopped chipotle peppers. To tone down the spice, use sweet Italian sausage in place of the chorizo.

# BRUSCHETTA SEA BASS WITH GARLIC GREEN BEANS

## SERVES 2

While sea bass is suggested, any firm white fish can be used in this quick, easy, and elegant dish for two. Bruschetta is a lot like a Mediterranean tomato salsa that makes the perfect topping for the delicate fish.

## 1. TOSS IT!

**Pressure Cooker**
Place green beans, wine, garlic, salt, and pepper into cooker and toss to combine. Place a steamer insert over the top and add the fish fillets. Pour lemon juice and zest over fish, and lightly season with salt and pepper before topping with bruschetta.

**Slow Cooker**
Place green beans, wine, garlic, salt, and pepper into cooker, and toss to combine. Place the fish fillets over green beans. Squeeze lemon over fish and lightly season with salt and pepper before topping with bruschetta.

## 2. COOK IT!

**Pressure Cooker**
Lock lid, close pressure valve, and set to HIGH for 4 minutes. Open pressure valve to quickly release the pressure.

**Slow Cooker**
Cover and set to LOW for 2½ hours, or until fish is flaky and warm throughout.

## 3. GO!

Serve the fish fillets alongside or over the green beans.

## INGREDIENTS:

10 ounces frozen green beans

¾ cup dry white wine

1 tablespoon minced garlic

½ teaspoon salt

½ teaspoon black pepper

2 frozen skin-off sea bass fillets

Juice of 1 lemon

Zest of half a lemon

½ cup prepared bruschetta

2 tablespoons butter

**ERIC'S TIP:** Fresh bruschetta can usually be purchased in the deli section near refrigerated salsas. You can also find it in small jars in the pasta aisle.

# CEDAR PLANK GROUPER

## SERVES 3

## 1. TOSS IT!

Place potatoes, kielbasa, clam juice, dill, butter, garlic, salt, and pepper into desired cooker, tossing to combine. Top the potatoes with the soaked cedar plank, then arrange fish fillets over plank. Season lightly with the crab seasoning.

## 2. COOK IT!

**Pressure Cooker**
Top the potatoes with the soaked cedar plank, then arrange fish fillets over plank. Season lightly with the crab seasoning. Lock lid, close pressure valve, and set to HIGH for 6 minutes. Open pressure valve to quickly release the pressure.

**Slow Cooker**
Cover and set to HIGH for 2 hours. Top the potatoes with the soaked cedar plank, then arrange fish fillets over plank. Season lightly with the crab seasoning. Switch cooker to LOW and cook an additional 2 hours, or until fish is flaky and warm throughout.

## 3. GO!

Serve the fish fillets alongside the fingerling potatoes.

**ERIC'S TIP:** You can easily substitute salmon, swordfish, or any large flaky fish. Adding a few threads of saffron will give this the scent of Bouillabaisse.

## INGREDIENTS:

1½ pounds small fingerling potatoes

½ pound kielbasa sausage, sliced

1 cup clam juice

4 tablespoons chopped fresh dill

2 tablespoons butter

1 tablespoon chopped garlic

½ teaspoon salt

1 teaspoon black pepper

1 cedar plank, soaked in water

3 (6-ounce) frozen grouper fillets

Maryland crab seasoning

# POTATO & VEGETABLE

LENTIL AND SWEET POTATO STEW

RATATOUILLE

MAPLE-CANDIED YAMS

CHEESY BROCCOLI

BUFFALO CAULIFLOWER

BROCCOLI CHEDDAR RICE

LOADED MASHED POTATOES

FRENCH ONION GREEN BEANS

# LENTIL AND SWEET POTATO STEW

## SERVES 6

This vegetarian stew is not only packed with flavor, but also features protein-rich lentils. For even more superfood goodness, try tossing in a few handfuls of chopped kale.

## 1. TOSS IT!

Place all ingredients, except parsley, into desired cooker, stirring to combine.

## 2. COOK IT!

**Pressure Cooker**
Lock lid, close pressure valve, and set to HIGH for 5 minutes. Let the pressure release naturally for 10 minutes before opening valve to release remaining pressure.

**Slow Cooker**
Cover and set to LOW for 8 hours.

## 3. GO!

Serve garnished with chopped fresh parsley.

**ERIC'S TIP:** For a nice contrast, top each bowl of stew with a drizzle of heavy cream or a dollop of sour cream.

## INGREDIENTS:

1 pound dried lentils, rinsed

6½ cups vegetable stock

2 sweet potatoes, peeled and chopped

1 cup diced yellow onion

½ cup diced celery

1 tablespoon olive oil

2 teaspoons minced garlic

2 bay leaves

1 teaspoon cumin

1 teaspoon coriander

2 teaspoons sugar

1 teaspoon lemon juice

1¼ teaspoons salt

1 teaspoon black pepper

Chopped fresh parsley, for garnish

# RATATOUILLE

## SERVES 4

To develop deep flavors, Ratatouille can often require the skills and prep-work of a trained chef. However, this recipe is as simple as tossing and… going.

## 1. TOSS IT!

Place all ingredients into desired cooker, tossing to combine.

## 2. COOK IT!

**Pressure Cooker**
Lock lid, close pressure valve, and set to HIGH for 4 minutes. Open pressure valve to quickly release the pressure.

**Slow Cooker**
Cover and set to LOW for 6 hours, or until vegetables are very tender.

## 3. GO!

Serve immediately.

**ERIC'S TIP:** For vegetables that are so tender that they fall apart, cut into 1-inch pieces. For slightly firmer vegetables, cut into larger 1½-inch pieces.

## INGREDIENTS:

1 eggplant, large chopped

2 yellow squash, large chopped

2 zucchini, large chopped

2 tomatoes, large chopped

1 green bell pepper, large chopped

1 cup prepared pasta sauce

½ cup vegetable stock

2 teaspoons balsamic vinegar

2 teaspoons sugar

2 teaspoons dried oregano

2 teaspoons minced garlic

¾ teaspoon onion powder

¾ teaspoon salt

½ teaspoon black pepper

# MAPLE-CANDIED YAMS

## SERVES 4

Tender candied yams (which are actually just sweet potatoes) don't just come from a can. Making them from scratch is not only satisfying, but so much better-tasting. My simple recipe infuses the yams with the flavors of orange juice and cinnamon, before tossing in maple syrup and butter to candy them.

## 1. TOSS IT!

Place water, orange juice, and cinnamon into your desired cooker.

## 2. COOK IT!

**Pressure Cooker**
Place a steamer insert into the pressure cooker and arrange sweet potatoes over the top. Lock lid, close pressure valve, and set to HIGH for 4 minutes. Open pressure valve to quickly release the pressure.

**Slow Cooker**
Toss sweet potatoes in the liquid in the cooker. Cover and set to LOW for 4 hours.

## 3. GO!

Drain all liquid from cooker. Toss cooked sweet potatoes in maple syrup, butter, and salt before serving.

### INGREDIENTS:

½ cup water

½ cup orange juice

1 teaspoon ground cinnamon

3 large sweet potatoes, peeled and cut into 1¼-inch chunks

⅓ cup maple syrup

2 tablespoons butter

¼ teaspoon salt

**ERIC'S TIP:** The orange juice infuses the potatoes with even more flavor, however it can be omitted to cut down on your shopping list.

# CHEESY BROCCOLI

## SERVES 4–6

## 1. TOSS IT!

Place broccoli, chicken stock, butter, garlic, salt, and pepper into desired cooker and toss to combine.

## 2. COOK IT!

**Pressure Cooker**
Lock lid, close pressure valve, and set to HIGH for 3 minutes. Open pressure valve to quickly release the pressure. Stir in Alfredo sauce.

**Slow Cooker**
Stir in Alfredo sauce. Cover and set to HIGH for 2 hours, just until broccoli is tender.

## 3. GO!

Stir in cheddar and Parmesan cheeses before serving.

**ERIC'S TIP:** If the cheeses aren't fully melting when stirred into the slow cooker, simply cover and let cook an additional 10 minutes.

## INGREDIENTS:

3 crowns broccoli, cut into large florets

½ cup chicken stock

2 tablespoons butter

1 tablespoon chopped garlic

1 teaspoon black pepper

1 cup prepared Alfredo sauce

1 cup shredded cheddar cheese

¼ cup grated Parmesan cheese

salt, if needed, to taste

# BUFFALO CAULIFLOWER

## SERVES 4-6

## 1. TOSS IT!

Place all ingredients, except bleu cheese, into desired cooker.

## 2. COOK IT!

**Pressure Cooker**
Lock lid, close pressure valve, and set to LOW for 2 minutes. Open pressure valve to quickly release the pressure.

**Slow Cooker**
Cover and set to LOW for 2 hours.

## 3. GO!

Stir in crumbled bleu cheese to thicken before serving.

### INGREDIENTS:

Florets of 1 large head cauliflower

1 tablespoon chopped garlic

1 cup buffalo sauce

3 tablespoons butter

1 cup chopped celery

1 cup chopped carrots

1 teaspoon salt

1 teaspoon pepper

½ cup crumbled bleu cheese

**ERIC'S TIP:** To reduce the heat, simply reduce the buffalo sauce down to ¾ cup, then stir in a tablespoon of honey and 2 additional tablespoons of butter in step 3.

# BROCCOLI CHEDDAR RICE

## SERVES 4

This creamy, cheesy rice is a family-favorite combination of flavors, much fresher than boxed rice mixes you'd find in the store. For a full meal, cubed ham can be added before or after cooking.

## 1. TOSS IT!

Place all ingredients, except cheddar cheese, into desired cooker and toss to combine.

## 2. COOK IT!

**Pressure Cooker**
Lock lid, close pressure valve, and set to HIGH for 6 minutes. Open pressure valve to quickly release the pressure.

**Slow Cooker**
Cover and set to HIGH for 2 hours, or until rice is tender.

## 3. GO!

Stir in cheddar cheese before serving.

**ERIC'S TIP:** Fresh or frozen broccoli florets can be used in this recipe.

## INGREDIENTS:

1¼ cups long grain white rice

12 ounces broccoli florets

2 cups chicken stock

1 cup whole milk

1 cup diced yellow onion

1 teaspoon onion powder

2 tablespoons butter

1 teaspoon salt

½ teaspoon black pepper

1½ cups shredded sharp cheddar cheese

# LOADED MASHED POTATOES

## SERVES 4–6

## 1. TOSS IT!

Place potatoes, chicken stock, butter, garlic, salt, and pepper into desired cooker, tossing to combine.

## 2. COOK IT!

**Pressure Cooker**
Lock lid, close pressure valve, and set to HIGH for 8 minutes. Open pressure valve to quickly release the pressure.

**Slow Cooker**
Cover and set to LOW for 6 hours, or until potatoes are tender.

## 3. GO!

Add cream cheese and use a potato masher to mash until smooth. Fold in bacon, cheddar cheese, Romano cheese, and chives before serving.

## INGREDIENTS:

3 pounds Yukon gold potatoes, cut into 2-inch pieces

½ cup chicken stock

3 tablespoons butter

1 tablespoon chopped garlic

1 teaspoon salt

1 teaspoon black pepper

4 ounces cream cheese

1 cup chopped cooked bacon

1 cup shredded cheddar cheese

½ cup grated Romano cheese

¼ cup chopped chives

1 seeded jalapeño pepper (optional)

**ERIC'S TIP:** Get creative with this recipe! I'll mix in cooked chorizo, cilantro, and queso fresco for Mexican potatoes, or crispy pancetta, sundried tomatoes, basil, and Gorgonzola for Italian potatoes!

# FRENCH ONION GREEN BEANS

## SERVES 4-6

This Toss and Go side dish has all the flavors of a traditional green bean casserole, without all the prep-work. Even more importantly, it uses real, fresh ingredients, not canned soup and canned fried onions.

## 1. TOSS IT!

Place all ingredients, except cream cheese and bread crumbs, into desired cooker, tossing to combine.

## 2. COOK IT!

**Pressure Cooker**
Lock lid, close pressure valve, and set to HIGH for 2 minutes. Open pressure valve to quickly release the pressure.

**Slow Cooker**
Cover and set to LOW for 4 hours, or until green beans are tender.

## 3. GO!

Drain ½ of the liquid from the cooker and then stir in cream cheese. Top with bread crumbs before serving.

**ERIC'S TIP:** Frozen green beans can also be used in this recipe without any adjustment to the cooking time.

### INGREDIENTS:

1 yellow onion, thinly sliced

24 ounces green beans, ends snipped

½ cup beef stock

2 tablespoons butter

2 teaspoons minced garlic

1 teaspoon onion powder

¾ teaspoon salt

¾ teaspoon black pepper

4 ounces cream cheese, softened

½ cup Italian seasoned bread crumbs

# DESSERTS

NEW YORK-STYLE CHEESECAKE

MIXED BERRY BREAKFAST AND SUNDAE SYRUP

PUMPKIN PIE CHEESECAKE

KEY LIME PIE CUPS

GRAHAM CRACKER "FRIED" APPLES

DOUBLE CHOCOLATE FLAN

MALLOW NUTTER BREAD PUDDING

CRANBERRY POACHED PEARS

COCONUT RICE PUDDING WITH PLANTAINS

CHOCOLATE BOURBON RICE PUDDING

CAPPUCCINO RICE PUDDING

BLUEBERRY MUFFIN BREAD PUDDING

# NEW YORK-STYLE CHEESECAKE

## SERVES 6

## 1. TOSS IT!

Spray a 7-inch springform pan with nonstick cooking spray, then line bottom with a parchment paper circle. Using an electric mixer, beat cream cheese and sugar just until smooth. Add egg, egg yolk, vanilla extract, and lemon juice and continue beating just until combined into a batter. Spread the batter into the prepared springform pan, and cover with aluminum foil. Add 1 cup of water to your desired cooker and insert a rack to keep the pan out of the water. Place pan on rack. Combine graham cracker crumbs and melted butter, then set aside.

## 2. COOK IT!

**Pressure Cooker**
Cover spring form pan with aluminum foil. Lock lid, close pressure valve, and set to HIGH for 40 minutes. Let the pressure release naturally for 5 minutes before opening pressure valve to release any remaining pressure.

**Slow Cooker**
Wrap the inside of the slow cooker lid with a clean towel to soak up condensation and tightly press the wrapped lid over cooker. Set to HIGH for 2 hours, just until the center of the cheesecake has is jiggly, but mostly set.

## 3. GO!

Remove from cooker and gently pat down graham mixture on top of cheesecake. Cool on a wire rack for 1 hour, then refrigerate at least 4 hours. Remove sides of springform pan, place serving plate on top of cheesecake and invert. Remove bottom piece of springform pan and parchment paper before slicing to serve.

## INGREDIENTS:

Nonstick cooking spray

16 ounces cream cheese, softened

¾ cup sugar

1 large egg, room temperature

1 large egg yolk, room temperature

1½ teaspoons vanilla extract

½ teaspoon lemon juice

½ cup graham cracker crumbs

2 tablespoons melted butter

**ERIC'S TIP:** When pressure cooking, many springform pans are too tall to place atop the steamer insert. I simply place the pan atop a metal cookie cutter or jar lid to keep it above the water line.

# MIXED BERRY BREAKFAST AND SUNDAE SYRUP

## SERVES 6

## 1. TOSS IT!

Place all ingredients into desired cooker, tossing to combine.

## 2. COOK IT!

### Pressure Cooker
Lock lid, close pressure valve, and set to HIGH for 4 minutes. Open pressure valve to quickly release the pressure.

### Slow Cooker
Cover and set to HIGH for 2–3 hours, until berries have broken down into a syrup.

## 3. GO!

Serve warm or chilled.

**ERIC'S TIP:** This will keep refrigerated for up to 10 days, but also freezes well.

## INGREDIENTS:

12 ounces frozen mixed berries

½ cup cranberry juice cocktail

⅓ cup sugar

¼ teaspoon vanilla extract

# PUMPKIN PIE CHEESECAKE

## SERVES 4–6

## 1. TOSS IT!

Mix cream cheese and brown sugar well. Add egg yolk, salt, pumpkin spice, vanilla extract, pumpkin puree, and sweetened condensed milk. Combine butter and graham cracker crumbs, then press into the bottom of a 7 inch springform pan. Pour the pumpkin mixture into the pan and cover tightly with foil.

## 2. COOK IT!

**Pressure Cooker**
Place rack on bottom of pot and add 1 cup of water. Set spring form pan on rack. Lock lid, close pressure valve, and set to HIGH for 40 minutes. Open pressure valve to quickly release the pressure.

**Slow Cooker**
Place rack on bottom of pot and add 1 cup of water. Set baking dish on rack. Cover and set to LOW for 4 hours.

## 3. GO!

Cool on the counter for 10 minutes, then chill completely in the refrigerator for at least 1 hour.

**ERIC'S TIP:** Use crushed ginger snap cookies and sweet potato puree for a slightly different flavor profile.

## INGREDIENTS:

¾ cup cream cheese

½ cup brown sugar

½ tsp. salt

1 ½ tsp pumpkin pie spice

2 egg yolks

1 tsp. vanilla extract

1 ¼ cups pumpkin puree

½ cup sweetened condensed milk

¾ cup graham cracker crumbs

2 tbsp melted butter

# KEY LIME PIE CUPS

## SERVES 6

These personal-sized key lime pies are made easier by moving the crust to a simple crumble of graham crackers sprinkled over the top. This also reduces fat, as there's no need to use butter to create the crust.

## 1. TOSS IT!

Spray 4 (6-ounce) ramekins with nonstick cooking spray. Whisk together egg yolks and sugar until pale yellow. Whisk in condensed milk and key lime juice. Pour batter equally between each ramekin and cover tightly with aluminum foil.

## 2. COOK IT!

**Pressure Cooker**
Add 1 cup of water to the cooker and position a steamer insert. Place the ramekins atop the insert. Lock lid, close pressure valve, and set to HIGH for 15 minutes. Let the pressure release naturally for 10 minutes before opening valve to release any remaining pressure.

**Slow Cooker**
Place the ramekins directly into the bottom of the slow cooker and add enough water to bring the level halfway up the sides of each ramekin. Cover and set to HIGH for 2 hours.

## 3. GO!

Cool on a wire rack for 30 minutes, then refrigerate at least 3 hours before serving. Serve in the ramekins, topped with macadamia-graham mixture.

### INGREDIENTS:

Nonstick cooking spray

2 large egg yolks

2 teaspoons sugar

1 (14-ounce) can sweetened condensed milk

¼ teaspoon vanilla extract

⅓ cup key lime juice

½ cup crumbled graham crackers

3 tablespoons finely chopped macadamia nuts

**ERIC'S TIP:** Like any good Key Lime Pie, this is great when topped with whipped cream before sprinkling with the crumbled graham crackers.

# GRAHAM CRACKER "FRIED" APPLES

## SERVES 6

While fried apples are sometimes considered a side dish in the South (let's face it, they're pretty much the inside of an apple pie!) in this recipe, I've made them into a satisfying dessert by thickening the syrupy sauce with crushed graham crackers; it's like adding that missing pie crust. You've just got to top each bowl with a scoop of vanilla ice cream.

## 1. TOSS IT!

Place apples, apple juice, cinnamon, vanilla extract, and salt into desired cooker, tossing to combine.

## 2. COOK IT!

**Pressure Cooker**
Lock lid, close pressure valve, and set to HIGH for 2 minutes. Open pressure valve to quickly release the pressure.

**Slow Cooker**
Cover and set to LOW for 4 hours, or until tender.

## 3. GO!

Stir in graham crackers, brown sugar, and butter before serving.

**ERIC'S TIP:** 1 cup of boxed "graham cracker crumbs" can be used in place of the crushed crackers, however I like to break up the full crackers to leave some bigger pieces.

## INGREDIENTS:

4 red apples, peeled, cored, and cut into eighths

1 cup apple juice

2 teaspoons ground cinnamon

¾ teaspoon vanilla extract

Pinch salt

1¼ cups crushed graham crackers

½ cup light brown sugar

1 tablespoon butter

# DOUBLE CHOCOLATE FLAN

## SERVES 6

This rich, creamy chocolate custard is cooked in four individual dishes, because there's no way you'll want to share! Each dish has chocolate syrup at the bottom for even more decadence, but also to replicate the (far more difficult to make) caramel of traditional flan.

## 1. TOSS IT!

Spray 4 (6-ounce) ramekins with nonstick cooking spray and then coat the bottom of each ramekin with 1/2 tablespoon of the chocolate syrup. Whisk together all remaining ingredients and pour equally between ramekins. Cover each tightly with aluminum foil.

## 2. COOK IT!

**Pressure Cooker**
Add 1 cup of water to the cooker and position a steamer insert. Place the ramekins atop the insert. Lock lid, close pressure valve, and set to HIGH for 10 minutes. Open pressure valve to quickly release the pressure.

**Slow Cooker**
Place the ramekins directly into the bottom of the slow cooker and add enough water to bring the level halfway up the sides of each ramekin. Cover and set to HIGH for 2 hours.

## 3. GO!

Cool on a wire rack for 30 minutes, then refrigerate at least 3 hours before serving.

## INGREDIENTS:

Nonstick cooking spray

2 tablespoons chocolate syrup

1 cup evaporated milk

2 large eggs

½ cup sugar

2 tablespoons cocoa powder

1 teaspoon vanilla extract

**ERIC'S TIP:** Though you can eat these right out of the ramekins, for the best presentation, run a knife around the circumference of the flan to help release it from the dish, then invert onto a small dessert plate.

# MALLOW NUTTER BREAD PUDDING

## SERVES 4–6

## 1. TOSS IT!

Split buns and distribute peanut butter and marshmallow spread to make mini sandwiches. Layer buns on their sides in a 7-inch ceramic baking dish. Combine eggs, milk and vanilla, and pour over buns. Top with peanut butter chips. Cover tightly with foil.

## 2. COOK IT!

**Pressure Cooker**
Place rack on bottom of pot and add 1 cup of water. Set baking dish on rack. Lock lid, close pressure valve, and set to HIGH for 20 minutes. Open pressure valve to quickly release the pressure.

**Slow Cooker**
Place rack on bottom of pot and add 1 cup of water. Set baking dish on rack. Cover and set to LOW for 4 hours.

## 3. GO!

Let bread pudding rest for 5 minutes to cool slightly and set.

**ERIC'S TIP:** This treat is wonderful served warm with a scoop of chocolate ice cream!

### INGREDIENTS:

8-10 Hawaiian slider buns

1 cup peanut butter

1 cup marshmallow spread

3 eggs, beaten

1 cup milk

1 tsp. vanilla extract

1 cup peanut butter chips

# CRANBERRY POACHED PEARS

## SERVES 4

These tender pears are infused with the sweet bite of cranberry juice. Orange, vanilla, and cinnamon are added for even more complementary flavors in this light dessert that will fill you with warmth.

## 1. TOSS IT!

Place all ingredients into desired cooker except the cornstarch and water, tossing to combine.

## 2. COOK IT!

**Pressure Cooker**
Lock lid, close pressure valve, and set to HIGH for 2 minutes. Open pressure valve to quickly release the pressure.

**Slow Cooker**
Cover and set to LOW for 4 hours, or until pears are tender.

## 3. GO!

Remove the pears into a serving bowl. In a small mixing bowl, mix the cornstarch and water until combined and pour into the cooker to thicken the sauce if desired. Serve pears warm, drizzled with cranberry juice from the cooker.

**ERIC'S TIP:** I like to top this with a dollop of whipped cream in the core of each pitted pear half.

## INGREDIENTS:

4 Bartlett pears, peeled, cored, and halved

1½ cups cranberry juice cocktail

¼ cup light brown sugar

2 cinnamon sticks

Zest of ½ an orange

½ teaspoon vanilla extract

1 tablespoon cornstarch

2 tablespoons water

# COCONUT RICE PUDDING WITH PLANTAINS

## SERVES 6

This tropical rice pudding with sweet fried plantains gets all of its creaminess from coconut milk. I like to add just a bit of coconut extract to ramp up the coconut flavor, however it is also good without the extract, letting the subtler (and natural) flavor of the coconut milk shine.

## 1. TOSS IT!

Place rice, coconut milk, sugar, vegetable oil, coconut extract, and salt into desired cooker and toss to combine. Top with the frozen plantains.

## 2. COOK IT!

**Pressure Cooker**
Lock lid, close pressure valve, and set to HIGH for 9 minutes. Open pressure valve to quickly release the pressure.

**Slow Cooker**
Cover and set to LOW for 3 hours, or until rice is very tender.

## 3. GO!

Serve warm or chilled. Pudding will thicken as it cools. If pudding becomes too thick, thin with milk or water, to achieve your desired consistency.

**ERIC'S TIP:** Add a ½ cup of almonds and a ½ cup of chocolate chips at the end to make it taste like a popular candy bar.

## INGREDIENTS:

1¼ cups Arborio rice

2 (13.5-ounce) cans coconut milk

¾ cup heavy cream

⅓ cup sugar

1 teaspoon vegetable oil

½ teaspoon coconut extract, optional

Pinch salt

1 (11-ounce) package frozen ripe plantains (maduros)

# CHOCOLATE BOURBON RICE PUDDING

## SERVES 12–16

## 1. TOSS IT!

Place rice, milk, sugar, orange juice concentrate, and bourbon into desired cooker and toss to combine.

## 2. COOK IT!

**Pressure Cooker**
Lock lid, close pressure valve, and set to HIGH for 11 minutes. Open pressure valve to quickly release the pressure.

**Slow Cooker**
Cover and set to LOW for 3 hours, or until rice is very tender.

## 3. GO!

Fold in hazelnuts, chocolate, and orange zest, then cover loosely to let the pudding thicken as it cools slightly, only 10 minutes. Serve garnished with additional chopped hazelnuts and shaved chocolate, if desired.

### INGREDIENTS:

3 cups Arborio Rice

7½ cups whole milk

1 cup sugar

⅓ cup orange juice concentrate

3 tablespoons bourbon

Pinch salt

1 cup chopped roasted hazelnuts

4 ounces dark chocolate, finely chopped

Zest of one orange, chopped

**ERIC'S TIP:** Rice pudding is great served warm or cold. To reheat, microwave in 15-second intervals, just until warmed. If the pudding over-thickens, stir in milk to achieve your desired consistency.

# CAPPUCCINO RICE PUDDING

## SERVES 6

There's no need to choose between coffee or dessert with this coffee-infused indulgence. Instant coffee granules add a great flavor with ease, however, you can also substitute ⅔ cup of espresso or extra-strong coffee in place of the water in the recipe.

## 1. TOSS IT!

Place all ingredients into desired cooker and toss to combine.

## 2. COOK IT!

**Pressure Cooker**
Lock lid, close pressure valve, and set to HIGH for 10 minutes. Open pressure valve to quickly release the pressure.

**Slow Cooker**
Cover and set to LOW for 3 hours, or until rice is very tender.

## 3. GO!

Stir in heavy cream while still warm.  Serve warm or chilled. Pudding will thicken as it cools. If pudding becomes too thick, thin with milk or water to reach desired consistency.

**ERIC'S TIP:** Any short grain white rice can be used to make this, however Arborio tends to release more starch to thicken the pudding.

### INGREDIENTS:

1 cup Arborio rice

4 cups whole milk

½ cup brown sugar

1½ tablespoons instant coffee granules

1 teaspoon vegetable oil

¼ teaspoon ground cinnamon

1 teaspoon vanilla

½ cup heavy cream

Pinch salt

# BLUEBERRY MUFFIN BREAD PUDDING

## SERVES 6

This easy dessert has all the flavors of a warm, buttered blueberry muffin, which makes leftovers a perfect breakfast indulgence the next day. I like to serve this, whether it is for dessert or breakfast, drizzled with maple syrup.

## 1. TOSS IT!

Spray a 7-inch springform pan with nonstick cooking spray. In a mixing bowl, whisk together milk, eggs, sugar, butter, vanilla extract, and salt. Gently fold in bread and blueberries to create the pudding batter. Spread batter into the prepared pan and cover with aluminum foil.

## 2. COOK IT!

**Pressure Cooker**
Add 1 cup of water to the cooker and position a steamer insert. Place the springform pan atop the insert. Lock lid, close pressure valve, and set to HIGH for 25 minutes. Let the pressure release naturally for 10 minutes before opening pressure valve to release any remaining pressure.

**Slow Cooker**
Place the springform pan directly into the bottom of the slow cooker without adding any water. Cover and set to LOW for 3 hours, or until center of pudding is springy and set.

## 3. GO!

Cool on a wire rack for 5 minutes before slicing to serve warm. Or, refrigerate 4 hours to serve chilled.

### INGREDIENTS:

Nonstick cooking spray

1½ cups evaporated milk

6 large eggs

1 cup sugar

4 tablespoons butter, melted

3 teaspoons vanilla extract

Pinch salt

10 slices challah or potato bread, chopped

1 pint blueberries

**ERIC'S TIP:** This same recipe can be used with any combination of blueberries, raspberries, or blackberries.

# INDEX